W9-CKT-789

3 2109 00291 4688

JANUA LINGUARUM

STUDIA MEMORIAE
NICOLAI VAN WIJK DEDICATA

edenda curat

C. H. VAN SCHOONEVELD

Indiana University

Series Minor, 107

STUDIES ON SEMANTICS
IN
GENERATIVE GRAMMAR

by

NOAM CHOMSKY

1972
MOUTON
THE HAGUE · PARIS

LIBRARY OF CONGRESS CATALOG CARD NUMBER: 74-189711

Printed in Belgium by NICI, Printers, Ghent.

PREFACE

The three essays that follow take as their point of departure the formulation of grammatical theory presented in such work as J. J. Katz and P. M. Postal, *An Integrated Theory of Linguistic Descriptions,* 1964, and Chomsky, *Aspects of the Theory of Syntax,* 1965. For ease of exposition, I refer to this formulation as the "standard theory". The essays deal with problems that arise within this framework, and present a revision of the standard theory to an "extended standard theory" (EST). The status of deep structure is a central concern in all three essays. In the first, "Remarks on nominalization", the device of syntactic features is exploited to formulate the "lexicalist hypothesis" with regard to derived nominals, and evidence is presented indicating that this hypothesis is correct and that the properties of these structures can be appropriately expressed only in terms of the abstract concept "deep structure", in the sense of the standard theory and EST. The status of deep structure is discussed again in the third essay, where further evidence is presented leading again to the conclusion that a level of deep structure (in the sense of the standard theory and EST) must be postulated. The second essay is concerned with inadequacies of the standard theory, and a more refined theory of semantic interpretation is proposed, giving EST: the grammatical relations of the deep structure remain fundamental for syntactic interpretation, determining what have been called "thematic relations" or "case relations", but other aspects of meaning are determined by surface structure. The third essay develops EST further. Both the second and third essays compare EST with alternatives, in particular with the approach now often called "generative semantics", and present evidence that in the areas of difference, EST is to be preferred on methodological as well as empirical grounds. It is also argued that the areas of difference are more slight than much current work suggests and that many issues that appear to be significant in reality reduce to matters of terminology and notation, when clarified.

N. C.

ACKNOWLEDGEMENTS

Permission to reprint these articles from the following sources is gratefully acknowledged:

"Remarks on Nominalization" from *Readings in English Transformational Grammar*, Roderick A. Jacobs and Peter S. Rosenbaum (eds.) (Waltham, Mass.: Ginn and Co., 1970).

"Deep Structure, Surface Structure, and Semantic Interpretation" from *Studies in General and Oriental Linguistics Presented to Shiro Hattori on the Occasion of His Sixtieth Birthday*, Roman Jakobson and Shigeo Kawamoto (eds.) (Tokyo: TEC Co. Ltd., 1970).

"Some Empirical Issues in the Theory of Transformational Grammar" from *Goals of Linguistic Theory*, Stanley Peters (ed.) (Englewood Cliffs: Prentice-Hall Inc.).

CONTENTS

REMARKS ON NOMINALIZATION*

For the purposes of this paper, I will assume without question a certain framework of principles and will explore some of the problems that arise when they are applied in the study of a central area of the syntax of English, and, presumably, any human language.[1]

A person who has learned a language has acquired a system of rules that relate sound and meaning in a certain specific way. He has, in other words, acquired a certain competence that he puts to use in producing and understanding speech. The central task of descriptive linguistics is to construct grammars of specific languages, each of which seeks to characterize in a precise way the competence that has been acquired by a speaker of this language. The theory of grammar attempts to discover the formal conditions that must be satisfied by a system of rules that qualifies as the grammar of a human language, the principles that govern the empirical interpretation of such a system, and the factors that determine the selection of a system of the appropriate form on the basis of the data available to the language learner. Such a "universal grammar" (to modify slightly a traditional usage) prescribes a schema that defines implicitly the infinite class of "attainable grammars"; it formulates principles that determine how each such system relates sound and meaning; it provides a procedure of evaluation for grammars of the appropriate form. Abstractly, and under a radical but quite useful idealization, we may then think of language-learning as the process of selecting a grammar of the

* This work was supported in part by the U. S. Air Force [ESD Contract AF19(628)-2487] and the National Institutes of Health (Grant MH-13390-01).
[1] The presupposed framework is discussed in greater detail in a number of recent publications, specifically, J. Katz and P. Postal (1964); Chomsky (1965); and references cited there. For bibliographic references, see pp. 114-116.

appropriate form that relates sound and meaning in a way consistent with the available data and that is valued as highly, in terms of the evaluation measure, as any grammar meeting these empirical conditions.

I will assume that a grammar contains a base consisting of a categorial component (which I will assume to be a context-free grammar) and a lexicon. The lexicon consists of lexical entries, each of which is a system of specified features. The nonterminal vocabulary of the context-free grammar is drawn from a universal and rather limited vocabulary, some aspects of which will be considered below. The context-free grammar generates phrase-markers, with a dummy symbol as one of the terminal elements. A general principle of lexical insertion permits lexical entries to replace the dummy symbol in ways determined by their feature content. The formal object constructed in this way is a DEEP STRUCTURE. The grammar contains a system of transformations, each of which maps phrase-markers into phrase-markers. Application of a sequence of transformations to a deep structure, in accordance with certain universal conditions and certain particular constraints of the grammar in question, determines ultimately a phrase-marker which we call a SURFACE STRUCTURE. The base and the transformational rules constitute the syntax. The grammar contains phonological rules that assign to each surface structure a phonetic representation in a universal phonetic alphabet. Furthermore, it contains semantic rules that assign to each paired deep and surface structure generated by the syntax a semantic interpretation, presumably, in a universal semantics, concerning which little is known in any detail. I will assume, furthermore, that grammatical relations are defined in a general way in terms of configurations within phrase-markers and that semantic interpretation involves only those grammatical relations specified in deep structures (although it may also involve certain properties of surface structures). I will be concerned here with problems of syntax primarily it is clear, however, that phonetic and semantic considerations provide empirical conditions of adequacy that must be met by the syntactic rules.

As anyone who has studied grammatical structures in detail is well aware, a grammar is a tightly organized system; a modification of one part generally involves widespread modifications of other facets. I will make various tacit assumptions about the grammar of English, holding certain parts constant and dealing with questions that arise with regard to properties of other parts of the grammar.

In general, it is to be expected that enrichment of one component of the grammar will permit simplification in other parts. Thus certain descriptive problems can be handled by enriching the lexicon and simplifying the categorial component of the base, or conversely; or by simplifying the base at the cost of greater complexity of transformations, or conversely. The proper balance between various components of the grammar is entirely an empirical issue. We have no a priori insight into the "trading relation" between the various parts. There are no general considerations that settle this matter. In particular, it is senseless to look to the evaluation procedure for the correct answer. Rather, the evaluation procedure must itself be selected on empirical grounds so as to provide whatever answer it is that is correct. It would be pure dogmatism to maintain, without empirical evidence, that the categorial component, or the lexicon, or the transformational component must be narrowly constrained by universal conditions, the variety and complexity of language being attributed to the other components.

Crucial evidence is not easy to obtain, but there can be no doubt as to the empirical nature of the issue. Furthermore, it is often possible to obtain evidence that is relevant to the correct choice of an evaluation measure and hence, indirectly, to the correct decision as to the variety and complexity that universal grammar permits in the several components of the grammar.[2]

To illustrate the problem in an artificially isolated case, consider

---

[2] Needless to say, any specific bit of evidence must be interpreted within a fixed framework of assumptions, themselves subject to question. But in this respect the study of language is no different from any other empirical investigation.

such words as *feel*, which, in surface structure, take predicate phrases as complements. Thus we have such sentences as:

(1)   John felt angry (sad, weak, courageous, above such things, inclined to agree to their request, sorry for what he did, etc.).

We might introduce such expressions into English grammar in various ways. We might extend the categorial component of the base, permitting structures of the form noun phrase-verb-predicate, and specifying *feel* in the lexicon as an item that can appear in prepredicate position in deep structures. Alternatively, we might exclude such structures from the base, and take the deep structures to be of the form noun phrase-verb-sentence, where the underlying structure *John felt* [$_S$*John be sad*]$_S$ [3] is converted to *John felt sad* by a series of transformations. Restricting ourselves to these alternatives for the sake of the illustrative example, we see that one approach extends the base, treating *John felt angry* as a NP-V-Pred expression roughly analogous to *his hair turned gray* or *John felt anger* (NP-V-NP), while the second approach extends the transformational component, treating *John felt angry* as a NP-V-S expression roughly analogous to *John believed that he would win* or *John felt that he was angry*. A priori considerations give us no insight into which of these approaches is correct. There is, in particular, no a priori concept of "evaluation" that informs us whether it is "simpler", in an absolute sense, to complicate the base or the transformational component.

There is, however, relevant empirical evidence, namely, regarding the semantic interpretation of these sentences.[4] To feel angry is not necessarily to feel that one is angry or to feel oneself to be angry; the same is true of most of the other predicate expressions that appear in such sentences as (1). If we are correct in assuming that it is the grammatical relations of the deep structure that determine the semantic interpretation, it follows that the deep structure of (1) must not be of the NP-V-S form, and that, in fact,

---

[3]   Henceforth I shall use labeled brackets to indicate structures in phrase-markers; an expression of the form X[$_A$ Y]$_A$Z signifies that the string Y is assigned to the category A in the string XYZ.

[4]   There are a number of suggestive remarks on this matter in Kenny (1963).

the correct solution is to extend the base. Some supporting evidence from syntax is that many sentences of the form (1) appear with the progressive aspect (*John is feeling angry*, like *John is feeling anger*, etc.), but the corresponding sentences of the form NP-V-S do not (* *John is feeling that he is angry*). This small amount of syntactic and semantic evidence therefore suggests that the evaluation procedure must be selected in such a way as to prefer an elaboration of the base to an elaboration of the transformational component in such a case as this. Of course this empirical hypothesis is extremely strong; the evaluation procedure is a part of universal grammar, and when made precise, the proposal of the preceding sentence will have large-scale effects in the grammars of all languages, effects which must be tested against the empirical evidence exactly as in the single case just cited.

This paper will be devoted to another example of the same general sort, one that is much more crucial for the study of English structure and of linguistic theory as a whole.

Among the various types of nominal expressions in English there are two of particular importance, each roughly of propositional form. Thus corresponding to the sentences of (2) we have the gerundive nominals of (3) and the derived nominals of (4):[5]

(2)   a. John is eager to please.
       b. John has refused the offer.
       c. John criticized the book.
(3)   a. John's being eager to please
       b. John's refusing the offer
       c. John's criticizing the book
(4)   a. John's eagerness to please
       b. John's refusal of the offer
       c. John's criticism of the book

Many differences have been noted between these two types of nominalization. The most striking differences have to do with the

---

[5] The fullest discussion of this and related topics is in Lees (1960), from which I will draw freely.

productivity of the process in question, the generality of the relation between the nominal and the associated proposition, and the internal structure of the nominal phrase.

Gerundive nominals can be formed fairly freely from propositions of subject-predicate form, and the relation of meaning between the nominal and the proposition is quite regular. Furthermore, the nominal does not have the internal structure of a noun phrase; thus we cannot replace *John's* by any determiner (e.g., *that, the*) in (3), nor can we insert adjectives into the gerundive nominal. These are precisely the consequences that follow, without elaboration or qualifications, from the assumption that gerundive nominalization involves a grammatical transformation from an underlying sentencelike structure. We might assume that one of the forms of NP introduced by rules of the categorial component of the base is (5), and that general rules of affix placement give the freely generated surface forms of the gerundive nominal:[6]

(5)   [$_S$NP *nom* (Aspect) VP]$_S$

The semantic interpretation of a gerundive nominalization is straightforward in terms of the grammatical relations of the underlying proposition in the deep structure.

Derived nominals such as (4) are very different in all of these respects. Productivity is much more restricted, the semantic relations between the associated proposition and the derived nominal are quite varied and idiosyncratic, and the nominal has the internal structure of a noun phrase. I will comment on these matters directly. They raise the question of whether the derived nominals are, in fact, transformationally related to the associated proposi-

[6] I follow here the proposal in Chomsky (1965, p. 222) that the base rules give structures of the form NP-Aux-VP, with Aux analyzed as Aux₁ (Aspect), Aux₁ being further analyzed as either Tense (Modal) or as various nominalization elements and Aspect as (perfect) (progressive). Forms such as * *John's being reading the book* (but not *John's having been reading the book*) are blocked by a restriction against certain *-ing -ing* sequences (compare * *John's stopping reading, John's having stopped reading*, etc.). Tense and Modal are thus excluded from the gerundive nominal, but not Aspect. Nothing that follows depends on the exact form of the rules for gerundive nominalization, but I think that a good case can be made for this analysis.

tions. The question, then, is analogous to that raised earlier concerning the status of verbs such as *feel*. We might extend the base rules to accommodate the derived nominal directly (I will refer to this as the "lexicalist position"), thus simplifying the transformational component; or, alternatively, we might simplify the base structures, excluding these forms, and derive them by some extension of the transformational apparatus (the "transformationalist position"). As in the illustrative example discussed earlier, there is no a priori insight into universal grammar — specifically, into the nature of an evaluation measure — that bears on this question, which is a purely empirical one. The problem is to find empirical evidence that supports one or the other of the alternatives. It is, furthermore, quite possible to imagine a compromise solution that adopts the lexicalist position for certain items and the transformationalist position for others. Again, this is entirely an empirical issue. We must fix the principles of universal grammar — in particular, the character of the evaluation measure — so that it provides the description that is factually correct, noting as before that any such hypothesis about universal grammar must also be tested against the evidence from other parts of English grammar and other languages.

In the earliest work on transformational grammar (cf. Lees (1960)), the correctness of the transformationalist position was taken for granted; and, in fact, there was really no alternative as the theory of grammar was formulated at that time. However, the extension of grammatical theory to incorporate syntactic features (as in Chomsky (1965, Chapter 2)) permits a formulation of the lexicalist position, and therefore raises the issue of choice between the alternatives.[7] My purpose here is to investigate the lexicalist

---

[7] The transformationalist position is adopted in much recent work, for example, Lakoff (1965). It is argued in some detail in Chapin (1967). The lexicalist position is proposed in Chomsky (1965, pp. 219-220), but with the analysis of possessive subjects that is rejected here on p. 36; it is implicitly rejected, incorrectly, as I now believe, in Chomsky (1965, p. 184). A compromise position of the sort noted above is developed in detail by Langendoen (1967a). It is also discussed in Annear and Elliot (1965). Langendoen presents an analysis very much like the one that I will propose directly, and cites a good

position and to explore some of the consequences that it suggests
for the theory of syntax more generally.

Consider first the matter of productivity. As noted above, the
transformation that gives gerundive nominals applies quite freely.[8]
There are, however, many restrictions on the formation of derived
nominals. The structures underlying (6), for example, are transformed to the gerundive nominals of (7) but not to the derived
nominals of (8):

(6) a. John is easy (difficult) to please.
     b. John is certain (likely) to win the prize.
     c. John amused (interested) the children with his stories.
(7) a. John's being easy (difficult) to please
     b. John's being certain (likely) to win the prize
     c. John's amusing (interesting) the children with his stories
(8) a. * John's easiness (difficulty) to please
     b. * John's certainty (likelihood) to win the prize
     c. * John's amusement (interest) of the children with his
        . stories

There are, of course, derived nominals that superficially resemble
those of (8), for example, those of (9), which pair with the gerundive
nominals of (10):

---

deal of evidence in support of it. He refrains from adopting a full lexicalist
position because of such ambiguities as that of *proof* in *John's proof of the
theorem (took him a long time, is reproduced in the new text)*. However, this
objection to the full lexicalist hypothesis, for which I am responsible, seems to
me very weak. One might just as well suppose that a lexical ambiguity is
involved, analogous to the ambiguity of such words as *book, pamphlet*, etc.,
which can be either concrete or abstract *(the book weighs five pounds, ...was
written in a hurry)*, as was noted by Postal (1966*b*). See Note 11 in this
connection.

[8] There are certain restrictions. For example, the transformation is inapplicable
when the subject is of a type that does not permit possessives (e.g., * *that John
was here's surprising me*), and it often is very unnatural with verbs that involve
extraposition (* *it's surprising me that John was here*, * *John's happening to be
a good friend of mine*), although *it's having surprised me that John was here* and
John's happening to be there seem tolerable.

(9)   a. John's eagerness to please ((2a), (4a))
       b. John's certainty that Bill will win the prize
       c. John's amusement at (interest in) the children's antics
(10)   a. John's being eager to please ((2a), (3a))
       b. John's being certain that Bill will win the prize
       c. John's being amused at (interested in) the children's antics

These discrepancies between gerundive and derived nominals call for an explanation. Specifically, we must determine why the examples of (8) are ruled out although those of (9) are permitted.[9]

The idiosyncratic character of the relation between the derived nominal and the associated verb has been so often remarked that discussion is superfluous. Consider, for example, such nominals as *laughter, marriage, construction, actions, activities, revolution, belief, doubt, conversion, permutation, trial, residence, qualifications, specifications*, and so on, with their individual ranges of meaning and varied semantic relations to the base forms. There are a few subregularities that have frequently been noted, but the range of variation and its rather accidental character are typical of lexical structure. To accommodate these facts within the transformational approach (assuming, as above, that it is the grammatical relations in the deep structure that determine meaning) it is necessary to resort to the artifice of assigning a range of meanings to the base form, stipulating that with certain semantic features the form must nominalize and with others it cannot. Furthermore, the appeal to this highly unsatisfactory device, which reduces the hypothesis that transformations do not have semantic content to near vacuity, would have to be quite extensive.[10]

---

[9]   There is also at least one class of cases where the derived nominals are permitted but not the gerundive nominals, namely, examples where the gerundive is blocked because the subject does not possessivize (cf. Note 8). Thus the gerundive nominal *his negative attitude toward the proposal's disruption of our plans* is clumsy and *his bringing up of that objection's disrupting our plans* is impossible, but we can form the associated derived nominals: *the disruption of our plans by his negative attitude toward the proposal, ... by his bringing up of that objection.* We return to these cases directly.

[10]   The artificiality might be reduced by deriving nominals from underlying nouns with some kind of sentential element included, where the meaning can be

The third major difference noted above between gerundive and derived nominals is that only the latter have the internal structure of noun phrases. Thus we can have such expressions as *the proof of the theorem* (* *the proving the theorem*, with a gerundive nominal), *John's unmotivated criticism of the book* (* *John's unmotivated criticizing the book*), and so on. Correspondingly, the derived nominals cannot contain aspect; there is no derived nominal analogous to *John's having criticized the book*. Furthermore, many derived nominals pluralize and occur with the full range of

expressed in this way: for example, *John's intelligence* from *the fact that John is intelligent* (in *John's intelligence is undeniable*), and from *the extent to which John is intelligent* (in *John's intelligence exceeds his foresight*). It is difficult to find a natural source for the nominal, however, in such sentences as *John's intelligence is his most remarkable quality*. This idea runs into other difficulties. Thus we can say *John's intelligence, which is his most remarkable quality, exceeds his foresight;* but the appositive clause, on this analysis, would have to derive from * *the extent to which John is intelligent is his most remarkable quality*, since in general the identity of structure required for appositive clause formation to take place goes even beyond identity of the given phrase-markers, as was pointed out by Lees (1960, p. 76). Many open questions regarding recoverability of deletion in erasure transformations arise as this problem is pursued. For some discussion, see Chomsky (1965, pp. 145f., 179f.). Ross (1967); and Chomsky (1968). Ross (1967) suggests (Chapter 3, *n.* 19) that identity of base structures is required for erasure.

The scope of the existing subregularities, I believe, has been considerably exaggerated in work that takes the transformationalist position. For example, Lakoff (1965) gives what are probably the strongest cases for this position, but even of these very few are acceptable on the semantic grounds that he proposes as justifying them. Thus *John's deeds* does not have the same meaning as *things which John did* (p. IV-2), but rather, *fairly significant things which John did* (we would not say that one of John's first deeds this morning was to brush his teeth). We cannot derive *John's beliefs* from *what John believes* (p. V-23), because of such sentences as *John's beliefs are not mutually consistent, ... are numerous,* etc., or *John's beliefs, some of which are amazing,...*; nor can we derive it from *the things that John believes*, since the semantic interpretation will then be incorrect in such expressions as *I respect John's beliefs* or *John's beliefs are intense*. It is difficult to see how one can transformationally relate *I read all of John's writings* to *I read all of what John wrote*, in view of such expressions as *I read all of John's critical writings*, etc. And if one is to postulate an abstract verb *poetize* underlying *John's poems*, then what about *John's book reviews, dialogues, sonnets, limericks, Alexandrines*, etc.? In general, there are few cases where problems of this sort do not arise. Correspondingly, the transformationalist position is impossible to support, and difficult even to maintain, on semantic grounds.

determiners (*John's three proofs of the theorem, several of John's proofs of the theorem*, etc.). And derived nominals, in fact, can appear freely in the full range of noun phrase structures. For example, the sentence *John gave Bill advice* is just like any other indirect object structure in that it has the double passive (*advice was given (to) Bill, Bill was given advice*). It is difficult to see how a transformational approach to derived nominals can account for the fact that the structures in which they appear as well as their internal structure and, often, morphological properties, are those of ordinary noun phrases. None of these problems arises, as noted earlier, in the case of gerundive nominals.

These properties of derived nominals are quite consistent with a lexicalist approach and, in part, can even be explained from this point of view. Before going into this matter, let us elaborate the lexicalist position in slightly greater detail.

I noted earlier that the lexicalist position was not formulable within the framework of syntactic theory available at the time of Lees's work on nominalizations. The problem was that the obvious generalizations concerning the distributional properties of the base and derived forms were expressible, in that framework, only in terms of grammatical transformations. There was no other way to express the fact that the contexts in which *refuse* appears as a verb and *refusal* as a noun are closely related. However, when the lexicon is separated from the categorial component of the base and its entries are analyzed in terms of contextual features, this difficulty disappears. We can enter *refuse* in the lexicon as an item with certain fixed selectional and strict subcategorization features, which is free with respect to the categorial features [noun] and [verb]. Fairly idiosyncratic morphological rules will determine the phonological form of *refuse, destroy*, etc., when these items appear in the noun position. The fact that *refuse* takes a noun phrase complement or a reduced sentential complement and *destroy* only a noun phrase complement, either as a noun or as a verb, is expressed by the feature structure of the "neutral" lexical entry, as are selectional properties. Details aside, it is clear that syntactic features provide a great deal of flexibility for the expression of generalizations regarding distributional similarities. Hence what was a decisive objection to the lexicalist position no longer has any force.

Let us propose, then, as a tentative hypothesis, that a great many items appear in the lexicon with fixed selectional and strict subcategorization features, but with a choice as to the features associated with the lexical categories noun, verb, adjective. The lexical entry may specify that semantic features are in part dependent on the choice of one or another of these categorial features. This is, of course, the typical situation within the lexicon; in general, lexical entries involve certain Boolean conditions on features, expressing conditional dependencies of various sorts.[11] Insofar as there are regularities (cf. Note 10), these can be expressed by redundancy rules in the lexicon.

Consider now the problem of productivity noted above, specifically, the fact that we cannot form the derived nominals (8) corresponding to the sentences (6), although the structures underlying (6) can be transformed to the gerundive nominals (7), and we can form the derived nominals (9) associated with the gerundive nominals (10).

Consider first the examples *John is easy to please, John is eager to please,* only the second of which is associated with a derived nominal. This consequence follows immediately from the lexicalist hypothesis just formulated, when we take into account certain properties of the items *eager* and *easy.* Thus *eager* must be introduced into the lexicon with a strict subcategorization feature indicating that it can take a sentential complement, as in *John is*

[11]   It is immaterial for present purposes whether a lexical entry is regarded as a Boolean function of specified features or is to be replaced by a set of lexical entries, each of which consists of a set of specified features. It is unclear whether these approaches to problems of range of meaning and range of function are terminological variants, or are empirically distinguishable. Some of the matters touched on in Note 10 may be relevant. Consider, for example, the ambiguity of *book* and *proof* mentioned in Note 7. Certain conditions on recoverability of deletion would lead to the conclusion that a single lexical entry is involved when two senses of the word can be combined in apposition. Under this assumption, the choice between the alternatives just mentioned in the case of *book* and *proof* would be determined by the status of such sentences as *this book, which weighs five pounds, was written in a hurry* and *John's proof of the theorem, which took him a long time, is reproduced in the new text.*

eager (for us) to please. In the simplest case, then, it follows that in the noun position, *eager* will appear in the contexts *John's eagerness (for us) to please*, etc., with no further comment necessary. But *easy* (or *difficult*) does not appear in the lexicon with such a feature. There is no structure of the form ... *easy (difficult) S* generated by base rules. Rather, *easy (difficult)* appears in base phrase-markers as an adjective predicated of propositions as subject (*(for us) to please John is easy*, etc.); forms such as *it is easy (for us) to please John* are derived by extra-position.[12] Consequently, *easy* (or *difficult*) cannot be introduced by lexical insertion into the noun position with sentential complements, and we cannot derive such forms as (8a), * *John's easiness (difficulty) to please.* No such restriction holds for gerundive nominalization, which, being a transformation, is applicable to transforms as well as to base phrase-markers.

Consider next the examples * *John's certainty to win the prize* (= (8b)), *John's certainty that Bill will win the prize* (= (9b)). Again, the lexicalist hypothesis provides an explanation for this distinction between the two senses of *certain*. The sentence *John is certain to win the prize* is derived by extraposition and pronoun replacement from a deep structure in which *certain* is predicated of the proposition *John - to win the prize*, as is clear from the meaning.[13] In this sense, *certain* does not permit a propositional complement; it therefore follows from the lexicalist hypothesis that there cannot be a derived nominal *certainty to win the prize*, in this sense. But *John is certain that Bill will win the prize* derives from *John is certain [sBill will win the prize]s*. In the sense of *certain* in which it is predicated of a person, a propositional complement can be adjoined in the base. Consequently, the lexicalist hypothesis permits the associated derived nominal *John's certainty that Bill will win the prize*, generated by lexical insertion of *certain* in the noun position before a sentential complement.

Consider now examples (6c) through (10c). If derived nominals are formed by transformation, there is no reason why * *John's*

---

12   For discussion, see Rosenbaum (1967), and Kiparsky and Kiparsky (1967).
13   See references of Note 12.

amusement of the children with his stories (= (8c)) should not be
formed from the proposition that underlies the gerundive nominal
John's amusing the children with his stories, just as *John's amusement
at the children's antics* (= (9c)) would, on these grounds, be derived
from the proposition that underlies the gerundive nominal *John's
being amused at the children's antics* (= (10c)). The discrepancy
would be accounted for if we were to adopt the lexicalist position
and, furthermore, to postulate that such sentences as *John amused
the children with his stories* are themselves derived from an underlying structure of a different sort. The latter assumption is not
unreasonable. Thus it is well-known that among the properties of
verbs of the category of *amuse, interest,* etc., is the fact that there
are paired sentences such as (11):

(11)   a. He was amused at the stories.
       b. The stories amused him.

The facts regarding derived nominals suggest that (11b) is derived
from a structure that involves (11a); this would account for the
similarities in semantic interpretation and distributional properties
of (11a) and (11b), and would also, on the lexicalist hypothesis,
account for the occurrence and nonoccurrence of derived nominals.[14] Although independent motivation for the assumption that
(11a) underlies (11b) is weak, there appears to be no counter-
evidence suggesting that (11b) underlies (11a). One might, for
example, derive (11b) quite plausibly from a "causative" construction with roughly the form of (12):

(12)   The stories [+ cause] [she was amused at the stories]$_s$

I return to such structures briefly below. There is some evidence in
support of the assumption that a causative construction exists in
English (cf. Chomsky (1965, p. 180); Lakoff (1965, Section 9)),[15]

---

[14] This solution is proposed by Lakoff (1965, p. A-15f.), but on the transformationalist grounds that he adopts, there is no motivation for it.
[15] There are many problems to be explored here. Notice, for example, that
John interested me in his ideas is very different from *John interested me with his
ideas* (both types of prepositional phrases occur in *John interested me in politics
with his novel approach*); only the latter is similar in meaning to *John's ideas*

and the operation that erases the repeated noun phrase in the embedded proposition of (12) is of a sort found elsewhere, for example, in the derivation of such sentences as *John used the table to write on, John used the pen to write (with), John used the wall to lean the table against*, etc., from *John used the table* [s*John wrote on the table*]s, and so on.

Other examples for which a causative analysis has been suggested fall into the same pattern, with respect to formation of derived nominals. Consider, for example, the transitive use of *grow* as in *John grows tomatoes*, which might plausibly be derived from a structure such as (12), with *the stories* replaced by *John* in the subject position and the embedded proposition being the intransitive *tomatoes grow*. But consider the nominal phrase *the growth of tomatoes*. This is unambiguous; it has the interpretation of *tomatoes grow* but not of *John grows tomatoes*. If the latter is taken as a base form, there should be an associated derived nominal *the growth of tomatoes* with the same interpretation, just as we have the derived nominal *the rejection of the offer* associated with the transitive verb phrase *reject the offer*. If, on the other hand, the sentence *John grows tomatoes* is derived from a causative construction, the corresponding derived nominal is excluded (though not,

---

interested me. A full analysis of these expressions will have to take into account instrumental phrases, concerning which there are numerous problems that have been discussed in a number of stimulating papers by Fillmore, Lakoff, and others.

The brief mention of causatives in Chomsky (1965) takes the main verb of (12) to be the verb *cause*, but the distinction between direct and indirect causation suggests that this cannot be correct. Lakoff (1966b) argues that the distinction between direct and indirect causation is a matter of use, not underlying structure; thus he argues that *a breeze stiffened John's arm* and *a breeze caused John's arm to stiffen* are generally used to indicate direct causation, while *a breeze brought it about that John's arm stiffened* and *a breeze made John's arm stiffen* are generally used to indicate indirect causation, but that actually either interpretation is possible, from which it would follow that the underlying verb could be taken to be *cause* in causative constructions. However, it does not seem correct to regard this simply as a distinction of use. Thus we can say *John's clumsiness caused the door to open (the window to break)* but not *John's clumsiness opened the door (broke the window)*. For some discussion of this matter, see Barbara Hall (1965).

of course, the corresponding nominalization *the growing of tomatoes* — we return to nominalizations of this type on p. 59). Hence the lack of ambiguity offers empirical support for a combination of the lexicalist hypothesis with the causative analysis, though not for either of these assumptions taken in isolation.

Summarizing these observations, we see that the lexicalist hypothesis explains a variety of facts of the sort illustrated by examples (6) through (10) [in part, in conjunction with other assumptions about underlying structures, such as (12)]. The transformationalist hypothesis is no doubt consistent with these facts, but it derives no support from them, since it would also be consistent with the discovery, were it a fact, that derived nominals exist in all cases in which we have gerundive nominals. Hence the facts that have been cited give strong empirical support to the lexicalist hypothesis and no support to the transformationalist hypothesis. Other things being equal, then, they would lead us to accept the lexicalist hypothesis, from which these facts follow.

If the lexicalist hypothesis is correct, we should expect that derived nominals will correspond to base structures rather than transforms. I will return to some problems, which may or may not be real, that arise in connection with this consequence of the lexicalist hypothesis. Notice, however, that there is other corroborating evidence. For example, there are many verbs in English that must be listed in the lexicon as verb-particle constructions (*look up (the information)*, *define away (the problem)*, etc.). These forms undergo gerundive nominalization freely (*his looking up the information, his looking the information up, his defining away the problem, his defining the problem away*). The derived nominals, in general, are rather marginal, and hence not very informative. However, it seems to me that the forms of (13) are somewhat preferable to those of (14.)[16]

(13) a.   his looking up of the information
      b.   his defining away of the problem

---

[16] It is not obvious that such forms as *the reading of the book* are ordinary derived nominals. I return to this matter briefly below.

(14) a. * his looking of the information up
      b. * his defining of the problem away

This consequence follows from the lexicalist assumption, if the forms of (13) are regarded as derived nominals (see Note 16).

Notice also that although gerundive nominalization applies freely to sentences with verb phrase adjuncts, this is not true of the rules for forming derived nominals. Thus we have (15) but not (16):[17]

(15) his criticizing the book before he read it (because of its failure to go deeply into the matter, etc.)

(16) * his criticism of the book before he read it (because of its failure to go deeply into the matter, etc.)

This too would follow from the lexicalist assumption, since true verb phrase adjuncts such as *before*-clauses and *because*-clauses will not appear as noun complements in base noun phrases.

The examples (15) and (16) raise interesting questions relating to the matter of acceptability and grammaticalness.[18] If the lexicalist hypothesis is correct, then all dialects of English that share the analysis of adjuncts presupposed above should distinguish the expressions of (15), as directly generated by the grammar, from those of (16), as not directly generated by the grammar. Suppose that we discover, however, that some speakers find the expressions of (16) quite acceptable. On the lexicalist hypothesis, these sentences can only be derivatively generated. Therefore we should have to conclude that their acceptability to these speakers results from a failure to take note of a certain distinction of grammaticalness. We might propose that the expressions of (16) are formed by analogy to the gerundive nominals (15), say by a rule that converts X-*ing* to the noun X *nom* (where *nom* is the element that determines

---

[17] This was pointed out to me by M. Kajita. Notice that *his criticism of the book for its failure* ... is grammatical. Presumably, *for* phrases of this sort are part of the complement system for verbs and nouns.

[18] I refer here to the distinction drawn in Chomsky (1965, p. 11f.). For the distinction between direct and derivative generation, see Chomsky (1965, p. 227, *n.* 2).

the morphological form of the derived nominal) in certain cases. There is no doubt that such processes of derivative generation exist as part of grammar in the most general sense (for some discussion, see *Aspects*, Chapter IV, Section 1, and references cited there). The question is whether in this case it is correct to regard (16) as directly generated or as derivatively generated, for the speakers in question. There is empirical evidence bearing on this matter. Thus if the expressions of (16) are directly generated, we would expect them to show the full range of use and meaning of such derived nominals as *his criticism of the book*. If, on the other hand, they are derivatively generated in the manner just suggested, we would expect them to have only the more restricted range of use and meaning of the expressions of (15) that underlie them. Crucial evidence, then, is provided by the contexts (17) in which the derived nominal *his criticism of the book* can appear, but not the gerundive nominals (15) (with or without the adjunct):

(17)   a. — is to be found on page 15.
       b. I studied — very carefully.

The fact seems to be that speakers who accept (16) do not accept (18) though they do accept (19):

(18)   a. *His criticism of the book before he read it* is to be found on page 15.
       b. I studied *his criticism of the book before he read it* very carefully.
(19)   a. *His criticism of the book* is to be found on page 15.
       b. I studied *his criticism of the book* very carefully.

If correct, this indicates that speakers who fail to distinguish (16) from (15) are not aware of a property of their internalized grammar, namely, that it generates (16) only derivatively, by analogy to the gerundive nominal. It would not be in the least surprising to discover that some speakers fail to notice a distinction of this sort. As we see, it is an empirical issue, and there is relevant factual evidence. This is a general problem that must be borne in mind when acceptability judgments are used, as they must be, to discover the grammar that is internalized. In the present instance, the lexicalist hypothesis receives convincing support if it is true that there are fundamentally two types of acceptability judgment: the first, acceptance of (19) but neither (16) nor (18); the second, acceptance of (19) and (16) but not (18). It is difficult to see how the transformationalist hypothesis could accommodate either of these cases.

Returning to the main theme, notice that aspect will of course not appear in noun phrases and therefore, on the lexicalist hypothesis, will be absent from derived nominals (though not gerundive nominals).

Consider next the adjectives that appear with derived nominals, as in *John's sudden refusal* or *John's obvious sincerity*. Two sources immediately suggest themselves: one, from relatives (as *John's aged mother* might be derived from *John's mother, who is aged*); another, from adverbial constructions such as *John refused suddenly, John is obviously sincere*. The latter assumption, however, would presuppose that derived nominals can be formed from such structures as *John refused in such-and-such a manner, John was sincere to such-and-such an extent*, etc. This is not the case, however. We cannot have * *John's refusal in that manner (in a manner that surprised me)* or * *John's sincerity to that extent*. Furthermore, adjectives that appear with derived nominals often cannot appear (as adverbs) with the associated verbs: for example, we have *John's uncanny (amazing, curious, striking) resemblance to Bill* but not * *John resembled Bill uncannily (amazingly, curiously, strikingly)*. We might propose to account for this by deriving *John's uncanny resemblance to Bill* from something like *the degree to which John resembles Bill, which is uncanny*. But this proposal, apart from the difficulty that it provides no way to exclude such phrases as * *their amazing destruction of the city* from *the degree to which they destroyed the city, which was amazing*, also runs into the difficulties of Note 10. Though there remain quite a number of interesting problems concerning adjectives in derived nominal (and many other) constructions, I see nothing that conflicts with the lexicalist hypothesis in this regard.

Evidence in favor of the lexicalist position appears to be fairly substantial. It is important, therefore, to look into the further consequences of this position, and the difficulties that stand in the way of incorporating it into the theory of syntax.

Suppose that such phrases as *eagerness (for John) to please, refusal of the offer, belief in a supreme being*, etc., are base noun phrases. Clearly, if this approach is to be pursued, then the rules of the categorial component of the base must introduce an extensive range of complements within the noun phrase, as they do within the verb phrase and the adjective phrase. As a first approximation, to be revised later on, we might propose that the rules of the categorial component include the following:

(20) a. NP → N Comp
      b. VP → V Comp
      c. AP → A Comp

(21) Comp → NP, S, NP S, NP Prep-P, Prep-P Prep-P, etc.

Is there any independent support, apart from the phenomena of derived nominalization, for such rules? An investigation of noun phrases shows that there is a good deal of support for a system such as this.

Consider such phrases as the following:[19]

(22) a. the *weather* in England
      b. the *weather* in 1965
      c. the *story* of Bill's exploits
      d. the *bottom* of the barrel
      e. the *back* of the room
      f. the *message* from Bill to Tom about the meeting
      g. a *war* of agression against France
      h. *atrocities* against civilians
      i. the *author* of the book
      j. John's *attitude* of defiance towards Bill
      k. his *advantage* over his rivals

---

[19] Langendoen (1967a) discusses a number of examples of this sort.

l. his *anguish* over his crimes
m. his *mercy* toward the victims
n. a *man* to do the job
o. a *house* in the woods
p. his *habit* of interrupting
q. the *reason* for his refusal
r. the *question* whether John should leave
s. the *prospects* for peace
t. the *algebra* of revolution
u. *prolegomena* to any future metaphysics
v. my *candidate* for a trip to the moon
w. a *nation* of shopkeepers

In each of these, and many similar forms, it seems to me to make
very good sense — in some cases, to be quite necessary — to regard
the italicized form as the noun of a determiner-noun-complement
construction which constitutes a simple base noun phrase. The only
alternative would be to regard the whole expression as a transform
with the italicized element being a nominalized verb or adjective,
or to take the complement to be a reduced relative clause. In such
cases as those of (22), neither alternative seems to be at all motivated, although each has been proposed for certain of these examples.
Space prevents a detailed analysis of each case, but a few remarks
may be useful.

The analysis of the head noun as a nominalized verb requires that
we establish abstract verbs that are automatically subject to
nominalization. This requires devices of great descriptive power
which should, correspondingly, be very "costly" in terms of a
reasonable evaluation measure.[20] Nevertheless, it is an interesting

---

[20] For example, such a device could be used to establish, say, that all verbs
are derived from underlying prepositions. If one wishes to pursue this line of
reasoning, he might begin with the traditional view that all verbs contain the
copula, then arguing that *John visited England* is of the same form as *John is
in England* (i.e., * *John is visit England*), where *visit* is a preposition of the
category of *in* that obligatorily transforms to a verb incorporating the copula.
Thus we are left with only one "relational" category, prepositions. To rule out
such absurdities, it is necessary to exclude the devices that permit them to be
formulated or to assign a high cost to the use of such devices.

possibility. Perhaps the strongest case for such an approach is the class of examples of which (22i) is an instance. It has been argued, quite plausibly, that such phrases as *the owner of the house* derive from underlying structures such as *the one who owns the house;* correspondingly (22i) might be derived from the structure *the one who *auths the book*, **auth* being postulated as a verb that is lexically marked as obligatorily subject to nominalization. However, the plausibility of this approach diminishes when one recognizes that there is no more reason to give this analysis for (22i) than there is for *the general secretary of the party, the assistant vice-chancellor of the university*, and similarly for every function that can be characterized by a nominal phrase. Another fact sometimes put forth in support of the analysis of these phrases as nominalizations is the ambiguity of such expressions as *good dentist (dentist who is a good man, man who is good as a dentist)*. But this argument is also quite weak. The ambiguity, being characteristic of all expressions that refer to humans by virtue of some function that they fulfill, can be handled by a general principle of semantic interpretation; furthermore, it is hardly plausible that the ambiguity of *good assistant vice-chancellor* should be explained in this way.

For some of the cases of (22), an analysis in terms of reduced relatives is plausible; for example, (22o). But even for such cases there are difficulties in this approach. Notice that there are narrow restrictions on the head noun in (22o). Thus we have the phrase *John's house in the woods* meaning *the house of John's which is in the woods;* but we cannot form *John's book (dog, brother,...) in the woods (on the table,...)*. If John and I each have a house in the woods, I can refer to his, with contrastive stress on *John's*, as *JOHN'S house in the woods;* if we each have a book on the table, I cannot, analogously, refer to his as *JOHN'S book on the table*. Such observations suggest that the surface structure of *John's house in the woods* is *John's - house in the woods*, with *house in the woods* being some sort of nominal expression. On the other hand, in a true reduced relative such as *that book on the table*, there is, presumably, no main constituent break before *book*.

The analysis as a reduced relative is also possible in the case of

(22r) and (22s). Thus we have such sentences as (23), with the associated noun phrases of (24):

(23)   a. The question is whether John should leave.
       b. The prospects are for peace.
       c. The plan is for John to leave.
       d. The excuse was that John had left.

(24)   a. the question whether John should leave
       b. the prospects for peace
       c. the plan for John to leave
       d. the excuse that John had left

Despite the unnaturalness of relative clauses formed in the usual way with (23) as the embedded proposition, one might argue that these are the sources of (24), as reduced relatives. Alternatively, one might argue that the sentences of (23) are derived from structures incorporating (24). The latter assumption is far more plausible however. Thus there are no such sentences as (25):

(25)   a. * The question whether John should leave is why Bill stayed.
       b. * The prospects for peace are for a long delay.
       c. * The plan for John to leave is that Bill should stay.
       d. * The excuse that John had left was that Bill should stay.

Under the reduced relative assumption, there is no reason why (25) should be ruled out. This would be explained, however, if we assumed that such sentences as (23) are derived from structures incorporating the base noun phrases (24); for example, it might be proposed that (23) derives from (26) by replacement of the unspecified predicate Δ by the complement of the subject noun:

(26) $[_{NP}$ Det N Comp$]_{NP}$ be $[_{Pred} \Delta]_{Pred}.$[21]

---

[21]   Still another possibility would be to take the underlying form to be $[_{NP}$Det N$]_{NP}$ be $[_{NP}$Det N Comp$]_{NP}$ (e.g., *the question is the question whether John should leave*), with the second occurrence of the repeated noun deleted, but this too presupposes that the Det-N-Comp structures are base forms, not reduced relatives.

Under this analysis, the copula serves as a kind of existential operator. Structures such as (26) are motivated by other data as well; for example, as the matrix structure for such sentences as *what John did was hurt himself*, which might be derived from [$_{NP}$ *it that John hurt John*]$_{NP}$ be [$_{Pred}$ Δ]$_{Pred}$, through a series of operations to which we return below. In any event, there is an argument for taking the forms of (24) to underlie (23), rather than conversely.

The structures (22), and others like them, raise many problems; they do, however, suggest quite strongly that there are base noun phrases of the form determiner-noun-complement, quite apart from nominalizations. In fact, the range of noun complements seems almost as great as the range of verb complements, and the two sets are remarkably similar. There is also a wide range of adjective complements (*eager (for Bill) to leave, proud of John*, etc.). Therefore, it is quite natural to suppose that the categorial component of the base contains rules with the effect of (20), (21), a conclusion which lends further support to the lexicalist assumption.

These observations, incidentally, considerably weaken the argument that verb and adjective are subcategories of a category "predicator", as has been suggested in recent syntactic work.[22] The argument based on distributional similarities of verbs and adjectives collapses when we recognize that nouns share the same distributional properties; thus the properties are simply properties of lexical categories. A number of other arguments that have appeared in support of this proposal fail for a similar reason. Thus it has been argued that verbs and adjectives can both be categorized as stative-active, so that we have such sentences as (27) in the case of actives, but not (28) in the case of statives:[23]

(27)   a. Look at the picture.
        b. Don't be noisy.
        c. What I'm doing is looking at the picture.
        d. What I'm doing is being noisy.

---

[22]   Cf., for example, Lakoff (1966), Appendix A.
[23]   Examples from Lakoff, (1966).

    e. I'm looking at the picture.

    f. I'm being noisy.

(28)   a. * Know that Bill went there.

        b. * Don't be tall.

        c. * What I'm doing is knowing that Bill went there.

        d. * What I'm doing is being tall.

        e. * I'm knowing that Bill went there.

        f. * I'm being tall.

At best, the logic of this argument is unclear. Suppose it were true that just verbs and adjectives crossclassify with respect to the feature active-stative. It would not follow that verbs and adjectives belong to a single category, predicator, with the feature $[\pm$ adjectival] distinguishing verbs and adjectives. From the fact that a feature $[\pm F]$ is distinctive in the categories X, Y, it does not follow that there is a feature G such that $X = [+ G]$ and $Y = [- G]$, and a category $Z = [\pm G]$. What is more, nouns are subdivided in an exactly parallel way. Thus alongside (27) we have *be a hero, what he's doing is being a hero, he's being a hero;* alongside of (28) we must exclude * *be a person,* * *what he's doing is being a person,* * *he's being a person,* etc. Again, the property in question is a property of lexical categories; the fact that the lexical categories noun, verb, and adjective share this property does not imply that they belong to a super-category. In fact, there is, to my knowledge, no convincing argument for a category including just verbs and adjectives (or, to take another traditional view, nouns and adjectives), although it is not excluded that some such subdivision may be correct. It is quite possible that the categories noun, verb, adjective are the reflection of a deeper feature structure, each being a combination of features of a more abstract sort. In this way, the various relations among these categories might be expressible. For the moment, however, this is hardly clear enough even to be a speculation.

    Returning to the main theme, a good case can be made that the lexical categories noun, adjective, and verb (whatever their further substructure may be) can appear in base forms with complements to form noun phrases, adjective phrases, and verb phrases. If this is correct, then it would be quite reasonable to expect that certain items might appear, with fixed contextual features, in more than one of these categories. The lexicalist analysis of derived nominals proposes that this expectation is fulfilled.

The lexicalist hypothesis faces additional problems, however. Consider the phrase *John's proof of the theorem*, as a typical illustration. According to the lexicalist hypothesis, the item *prove* appears in the lexicon with certain contextual features that indicate the range of complements it can accept and the choice of items that may appear in these associated phrases. Yet to be accounted for, however, is the possessive noun phrase *John's* and its relation to the head noun *proof*. It might be suggested that the possessive noun phrase derived from a relative clause with *have*, as *John's table* might derive from the structure underlying *the table* [s*John has a table*]s, along lines that have been frequently discussed. Thus the source of *John's proof of the theorem* would be, in this analysis, the structure underlying *the proof of the theorem that John has*. While not implausible in this case, this approach quickly runs into difficulties when extended. Thus to account for *John's refusal to leave, John's invention of a better mousetrap*, and many other forms, it would be necessary to postulate abstract verbs that obligatorily undergo certain transformations, a dubious move at best, as noted earlier.

An alternative would be simply to derive the possessive noun phrase itself as a base form. Suppose, tentatively, that the rules generating determiners in the base component are the following:[24]

(29) a. Det $\rightarrow$ (Prearticle of) Article (Postarticle)

      b. Article $\rightarrow$ $\left\{ \begin{array}{l} \pm\ \text{def} \\ \text{Poss} \end{array} \right\}$

[24] It is immaterial for the present discussion whether the structures to the right of the arrow are, indeed, base structures, or whether certain of them are derived from "deeper" or different structures. It is sufficient, for present purposes, to note that (30), or something sufficiently like it, is the general form of the determiner at some stage of derivation. What is crucial, for the present, is that the possessive noun phrase is being assigned the status of the article $\pm$ def, whatever this may be in the base structure.

The noun phrase *several of John's proofs of the theorem*, under this analysis, would have a structure of roughly the following form:

(30)

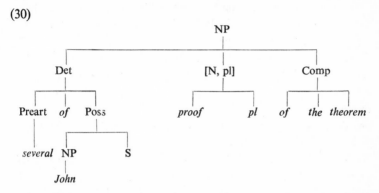

It would be analogous in structure, then, to the phrase *several of those proofs of the theorem*.

If this approach is correct, we would expect to find structures of the form NPs-N even where the N is not a derived nominal, and where the possessive construction in question does not derive from the corresponding structure: *N that NP has*. In fact, there is some evidence in support of this expectation. A number of people have noted that the distinction between alienable and inalienable possession, formally marked in certain languages, has a certain status in English as well. Thus the phrase *John's leg* is ambiguous: it can be used to refer either to the leg that John happens to have in his possession (alienable possession), that he is, say, holding under his arm; or to the leg that is, in fact, part of John's body (inalienable possession). But the phrase *the leg that John has* has only the sense of alienable possession. We cannot say that the leg that John has hurts or that it is weak from the climb, though we can make this statement of John's leg, in the inalienable sense of the phrase *John's leg*.[25] These observations lend plausibility to the view that *John's leg* has another source in addition to the structure underlying *the leg that John has*, from which it can be derived (in the

[25] These examples are due to John Ross.

alienable sense) along the same lines as *John's table* from the structure underlying *the table that John has*. The second source, then, might be given by the base rules (29), which are semantically interpreted as specifying inalienable possession. This assumption would account for the facts just noted.

Within the framework that I am here presupposing, grammatical relations are defined by configurations in the deep structure, and selectional features relate the heads of phrases that are associated in specific grammatical relations. Then the words *John* and *proof* are the heads of the related phrases *several of John's* and *proofs of the theorem* in *several of John's proofs of the theorem*, and the same selectional feature that associates subject and verb in *John proved the theorem* will relate these two items, despite the very different syntactic origin of the relationship.[26] We return to this matter later on. For the moment, it is sufficient to point out that by a suitable generalization of the interpretation of selectional features, we can account for the fact that the selectional relation of the possessive noun phrase of the determiner to the "verbal" head of the derived nominal is the same as that of the subject to the verb of the associated verb phrase. Hence in the simplest case, all of the contextual features of the items that appear as verbs in verb phrases and as derived nouns in derived nominals will be common to the two types of context.

It must be noted that only in the SIMPLEST case will exactly the same contextual (and other) features be associated with an item as a verb and as a noun. In general, lexical entries involve sets of shared features, organized in complex and little understood ways, and we should expect to find the same phenomenon in the case of derived nominals, given the lexicalist hypothesis. Examples such as (31) and (32) illustrate the discrepancy of contextual features that may be found in the case of certain noun-verbs.

(31)   a.   our election of John (to the presidency)

---

[26] If we take the structure in question to be, rather, (*several of* [(*John's*) (*proofs of the theorem*)]), the same conclusion follows, with respect now to the embedded phrase *John's proofs of the theorem*.

    b.   our belief in God

    c.   our consideration of John for the job

(32) a. * our election of John (to be) president

      b. * our belief in God (to be) omnipotent

      c. * our consideration of John (to be) a fool

Reactions to these sentences vary slightly; (31), (32) represent my judgments. Given such data, lexical entries must indicate that embedded sentences are not permitted in the complement to the nouns, although they are permitted in the complement to the associated verbs. Whatever generality there may be to this phenomenon can be extracted from individual lexical entries and presented in redundancy rules. This discrepancy in syntactic features between the noun and verb members of a noun-verb pair corresponds to the semantic discrepancies noted earlier (cf. p. 19) and like them, strengthens the lexicalist hypothesis. The appropriate device to rule out the sentences of (32) (while permitting (31)) is a lexical rule governing contextual features. To formulate such restrictions in the structure indices of transformations would be a rather complex matter.

Consider now some of the transformational rules that apply internally to complex noun phrases. Consider first such phrases as (33) through (36):

(33) a.   that picture of John's

      b.   a picture of John's

      c.   several of those pictures of John's

      d.   several pictures of John's

(34) a.   John's picture, several of John's pictures

      b.   the picture of John's that Bill painted

(35) a. * the picture of John's

      b. * several of the pictures of John's

(36)   * John's picture that Bill painted

The expressions of (35), (36) illustrate a systematic gap in this set. In general, expressions of the form *(prearticle of) the N of NPs* and *NPs N that S* are unnatural. The gaps illustrated by (35) and (36) are filled by (34a) and (34b), respectively.

Alongside the examples of (33) there is a superficially similar set in which *John's* is replaced by *John*: thus, *that picture of John*, etc. In this case, the phrases are presumably complex noun phrases with a "relational" head noun, like the examples of (22). The status of the analogues to (35) (namely, *the picture of John, several of the pictures of John)* is unclear. It is clear, however, that such phrases as *John's picture* (= (34a)) are ambiguous, meaning *the picture of John* or *the picture of John's*.

On just the evidence cited so far, one might propose various transformational analyses. Tentatively, let us suppose that there are three transformations, with roughly the effects of (37), (38), (39), applying in the order given:

(37)   *X-the-Y picture that John has* $\Rightarrow$ *X-John's-Y picture*
(38)   *X-John's-Y picture* $\Rightarrow$ *X-the-Y picture of John's*
(39)   *X-the-Y picture of John* $\Rightarrow$ *X-John's-picture*

X and Y are pre- and post-article (including the demonstrative element) respectively. There are problems in the formulation of such transformations to which we will return below. To account for the data presented above (38) will be obligatory when Y contains a demonstrative element (giving (33a), (33c), for example) or when the phrase contains a relative clause (preventing (36)), and will be blocked when Y is null, thus excluding (35).

Consider now such derived nominals as:

(40)   a. the destruction of the city
        b. the proof of it
        c. the murder of John

Rule (39) will apply, giving such transforms as *the city's destruction, its proof, John's murder*. The applicability of (39) to derived nominals varies in naturalness from case to case and from speaker to speaker, and must therefore be specified in part as an idiosyncratic property of lexical items, along the lines developed in Lakoff

(1965). In part, the applicability of (39) is determined by the character of the noun phrase of the complement, there being certain noun phrases that do not possessivize. Whatever the detailed restrictions may be, it seems clear that the operation in question extends to derived nominals as well as to complex noun phrases with "relational" head nouns. For convenience of reference, I will refer to rule (39) as the rule of *NP-preposing*.

Let us suppose, as suggested in the references of Note 1, that the underlying structure for passives is roughly *NP-Aux-V-NP-by* Δ, where *by* Δ is an agent phrase related, in ways that are still unclear in detail, to adverbials of means and manner. The passive operation, then, is an amalgam of two steps: the first replaces Δ by the subject noun phrase; the second inserts in the position vacated by the subject the noun phrase that is to the right of the verb. Let us refer to the first of these operations as AGENT-POSTPOSING. The second bears a close similarity to the operation of NP-preposing just discussed, and perhaps the two fall under a single generalization. If so, then the second component of the passive transformation can apply independently of the first, namely, as operation (39), internally to noun phrases. Whether or not this is so, we may inquire into the possibility that the operation of agent-postposing can apply independently of the second component of the passive transformation.

Pursuing this possibility, we note first that passivizability is a property of verbs — which is natural, given that V is the only lexical category mentioned in the structure index of the transformation. We can indicate this fact, along the lines of the references cited, by associating with certain verbs the contextual feature $[-$ by $\Delta]$ either as a lexical property (where it is idiosyncratic) or by a redundancy rule of the lexicon (where it is subject to some regularity). Assuming, as before, that the complements of nouns are the same in principle as those of verbs, we would expect to find in deep structures complex noun phrases of the form *Det-N-NP-by* Δ, for example, such phrases as *the enemy's-[destroy, + N]-the city-by* Δ. The word *destroy* will be spelled out phonologically as *destruction* in this case, and the preposition *of* inserted by a general rule applying to N-NP constructions.[27] Agent-postposing will then apply, as in the passive, giving *the destruction of the city by the enemy*. To provide this result, we need only extend the operation so that its domain may be a noun phrase as well as a sentence, a modification of the theory of transformations that is implicit in the lexicalist hypothesis; and we must somehow account for the appearance of the definite article in the transform, just as in the case of the transformation (38). A further modification is required by such phrases as *the offer by John*, which indicate, as is quite natural, that of the two components of the passive transformation, only NP-preposing and not agent-postposing requires the presence of an object (more generally, a noun phrase, as in the "pseudo-passives" *John was laughed at, ... approved of*, etc.) in the position following the verb.[28]

[27]   Alternatively, it has been proposed that the preposition is an obligatory part of the underlying noun phrase, and is deleted in certain contexts, for example, the context: verb —. This seems to me dubious, however. Notice that the preposition is not invariably deleted in the context verb — NP, for example in such cases as *approve of John*. Hence we would have to postulate an idio-syncratic feature *F* that subdivides verbs into those that do and those that do not undergo *of*-deletion. An arbitrary bifurcation of the lexicon is the worst possible case, of course. No such arbitrary feature is needed if we suppose the *of* to be introduced in the context N — NP. Of course *approve* will be distin-guished from *read* by the strict subcategorization features [— PP], [— NP] (or whatever variants of these are employed), exactly as *laugh* (*at John*) is distinguished from *see* (*John*); this, however, is not a new classification, but rather one that is necessary however the matter of *of* is handled. To make matters worse for the theory of *of*-deletion, the new, idiosyncratic feature *F* will have to cut across related senses of a single item, since we have *approve-the proposal* alongside of *approve-of the proposal*. Furthermore, there is a possibility, which should be explored, of combining the proposed rule of *of*-insertion with the rule governing placement of *of* in prenominal constructions such as *lots of work, several of the boys, a group of men*, etc. Such considerations suggest that the preposition is an inherent part of the prepositional phrase, but not of the object.
[28]   Such an analysis of the phrases in question is proposed by Kinsuke Hasegawa, "The Passive Construction in English", forthcoming in *Language*. Hasegawa suggests, furthermore, that the passive derives from a matrix structure containing the grammatical subject as object: thus *Bill was seen by John* would derive from something like *Bill is: John saw Bill*. Despite his arguments, I am skeptical about this proposal. A serious objection, it seems to me, is that there are phrases which can appear as grammatical subject only in

Notice that a verb which is not passivizable, such as *marry* (in one sense) or *resemble*, will not be subject to this operation as a derived nominal. Thus *John's marriage to Mary, John's resemblance to Bill* will not transform to *the marriage to Mary by John, the resemblance to Bill by John* (though *John's offer (of amnesty) to the prisoners* does transform to *the offer (of amnesty) to the prisoners by John*). For additional related observations, see Lees (1960). This is a confused matter, however, and conclusions cannot be drawn with any confidence.

We have now discussed two transformations that apply to complex noun phrases: agent-postposing, which gives *the destruction of the city by the enemy*, and NP-preposing, which gives *the city's destruction*. Agent-postposing is simply a generalization of one of the components of the passive transformation. NP-preposing is similar to, and may fall under a generalization of, the other component. Suppose now that we have an underlying deep structure of the form *Det-N-Comp*, where the determiner is a noun phrase (ultimately possessive, if it remains in this position) and the complement is a noun phrase followed by the agent phrase *by* Δ; for example, *the enemy-destruction-of the city-by* Δ. Applying agent-postposing, we derive *the-destruction of the city-by the enemy*, as before. If we now extend NP-preposing so that it can apply not only in the cases given before, but also before agent phrases, we derive, from the last-formed structure, the phrase *the city's destruction by the enemy*. It is important to see, then, that the latter phrase is only apparently the nominalization of a passive; if it were really the nominalization of a passive, this fact would refute the lexicalist hypothesis, since, as was emphasized earlier, it follows from this hypothesis that transforms should not undergo the

---

the passive construction. Thus we can have *a man to do the job was found by John* from *John found a man to do the job* [cf. (22n)], but such expressions as *a man to do the job came to see me* seem highly unnatural. Similarly, there are certain idioms that undergo passivization (cf. *Aspects*, p. 190f.) although the phrase that appears as grammatical subject cannot normally appear as a deep subject (*I didn't expect that offense would be taken at that remark, advantage was taken of John*, etc.). Such facts are difficult to reconcile with the proposal that the passive derives from a matrix proposition with an embedded complement.

processes that give derived nominals. In fact, one major empirical justification offered for the lexicalist hypothesis was that, in a number of otherwise puzzling cases, it is precisely this state of affairs that we discover. But we now see that the crucial phrases need not be regarded as nominals derived transformationally from the passive (with the auxiliary mysteriously disappearing), but can rather be explained as, in effect, passives of base-generated derived nominals, by independently motivated transformations.

Notice that agent-postposing is obligatory for certain subject noun phrases that do not permit formation of possessives. Since agent-postposing is unspecifiable for gerundive nominals, there are certain derived nominals with no gerundive counterpart, as pointed out in Note 9. Under the transformationalist hypothesis, there would be no more reason to expect agent-postposing in derived than in gerundive nominals. Hence an additional argument in support of the lexicalist hypothesis is that it provides this distinction on independent grounds.

It is possible that such derived nominals as *the necessity for John to leave, the likelihood that John will leave,* and so on might be derived by obligatory agent-postposing from the underlying noun phrases [*for John to leave*]'s *necessity,* [*that John will leave*]'s *likelihood.*

A minor transformational rule will replace *by* by *of* under certain conditions, permitting *the refusal to leave of those men* (or *the refusal of those men to leave)* alternating with *the refusal to leave by those men* (or *the refusal by those men to leave).* Presumably, it is this rule that applies in the case of the nominals *the growling of the lion,* etc. Some speakers apparently accept expressions such as *John's likelihood of leaving,* though to me these are entirely unacceptable. Perhaps such expressions can be derived, by an extension of NP-preposing, from *the likelihood of John leaving.* Such expressions as * *John's likelihood to leave* apparently are acceptable to no one, exactly as is predicted by the lexicalist hypothesis.

Implicit in the rules given so far is the possibility that there will be base noun phrases of the form *Det-N-NP by* Δ, where the head noun is not derived from an underlying stem that also appears as a verb, thus a case of the sort illustrated in (22). Of course, such a possibility will be realized as a well-formed surface structure only if the determiner is filled by a phrase which can ultimately appear in the agent position, replacing the symbol Δ, which will otherwise, through the filtering effect of transformations, mark the structure as not well formed. If it is true, as suggested above, that some form of "inalienable possession" is expressed by base rules generating noun phrases in the determiner position, then the possibility just sketched can be realized. That there may be structures of this sort is suggested by a fuller analysis of such phrases as *John's picture*, discussed briefly above. We noted that there are two interpretations of this phrase, one derived from the structure underlying *the picture that John has* by rule (37), and the other derived by NP-preposing, rule (39), from the complex noun phrase that would otherwise be realized as *the picture of John*. There is, however, still a third interpretation, namely, with the same meaning as *the picture that John painted*. Conceivably, this is the interpretation given to the base structure $[_{\text{Det}} \textit{John's}]_{\text{Det}} [_{\text{N}} \textit{picture}]_{\text{N}}$, with a generalization of the notion "inalienable possession" to a kind of "intrinsic connection". A similar triple ambiguity can be found in other cases, e.g., *John's story*, where John can be the subject of the story *(the story of John)*, the writer (intrinsic connection), or an editor proposing the story for publication at a meeting *(the story that John has)*. Notice that if *John's picture, John's story*, and so on are generated in the base with the sense of intrinsic connection, they will be subject to rule (38), giving *that picture of John's, those stories of John's, the story of John's that I told you about*, and so on, all with the meaning of intrinsic connection. The latter phrases will thus be two-way ambiguous, meaning *the picture that John has* or *the picture that John painted* (though not *the picture of John*), and so on. This is of course true, and gives some further support for the analysis proposed.

Now consider the base structure *Det-N-NP-by* Δ, where the determiner is realized in the base as the noun phrase *John*, the head noun as *picture*, and the noun phrase complement as *Mary*.

Without the agent phrase in the base structure, this will give *John's picture of Mary* (itself of course ambiguous, since another source could have been the structure underlying *the picture of Mary that John has*).[29] With the agent phrase generated in the base, the agent-postposing transformation must apply, giving *the picture of Mary by John*. Had the complement been omitted, we would derive *the picture by John*. Agent-postposing must precede the transformation of NP-preposing that gives *the city's destruction*, or we will derive *the destruction by the city* from *the-destroy-the city*. It therefore follows that *the picture (of Mary) by John* cannot be derived from the phrase *John's picture*, which is derived in turn from *the picture of John*. Hence *the picture of Mary by John* cannot have the latter meaning. Along these lines, a number of facts fall together in what seems a quite natural way.

Consider, finally, a slightly more complicated case, namely, a structure of the form: *Det-N-NP-by Δ-that NP has*, where the determiner is a possessivized noun phrase. An example would be (41):

(41)   Rembrandt's portrait of Aristotle by Δ that the Metropolitan Museum has.

Applying agent-postposing, we derive *the portrait of Aristotle by Rembrandt that the Metropolitan Museum has*. Rule (37) gives *the Metropolitan Museum's portrait of Aristotle by Rembrandt*. Rule (38) would then give the quite clumsy phrase *the portrait of Aristotle by Rembrandt of the Metropolitan Museum's*. This would be natural if the final phrase, *of the Metropolitan Museum's*, were omitted, in which case rule (39), NP-preposing, would then apply to give *Aristotle's portrait by Rembrandt*. Clearly, the rule of agent-

---

[29]   Notice, then, that the transformation (37) that gives *John's picture* from *the picture that John has* will also give *John's picture of Mary* from *the picture of Mary that John has*. The transformation therefore applies not to a structure of the form *Det-N-that NP has* but rather *Det-$\bar{N}$-that NP has*, where $\bar{N}$ represents the expression *picture of Mary* (in *the picture of Mary that John has*) or the expression *picture* (in *the picture that John has*). We return to the status of $\bar{N}$ below. On p. 32 we noted another situation in which the noun and its complement appear to form a single unit.

postposing must be permitted to apply before rule (37), which forms
NP's N from *the N that NP has*. Furthermore, the rule of agent-
postposing cannot apply after rule (37). If this ordering were
permitted, the underlying structure *the portrait of Aristotle by* Δ
that the Metropolitan has would become, by (37), *the Metropolitan's
portrait of Aristotle by* Δ, and then, by agent-postposing, *the
portrait of Aristotle by the Metropolitan*. Therefore the ordering of
the transformations we have been discussing must be: agent-
postposing, (37), (38), (39).

So far we have been exploring the possibility that complex noun
phrases, which ultimately will be possessivized if not removed from
the determiner by a transformation, are derived directly by base
rules such as (29). We have noted, however, that when the noun
phrase is removed from the determiner, an article may appear in
the position that it vacated. Thus we can have *the picture of Mary
by John, a picture of Mary by John, several pictures of Mary by
John, one of the pictures of Mary by John,* etc. These facts suggest
that rule (29b) is incorrect, and that it be replaced by something
like (42):

(42)   Article → [± def, (NP)]

The article, then, can be either definite or indefinite, or can be a full
noun phrase with the associated feature [+ definite] or [− definite].
When the noun phrase is removed from the determiner by a transformation, the feature [± definite] will remain, much as the feature
[+ PRO] remains in certain positions when a noun phrase is
removed. (Continuing with such an analysis, we would have to
stipulate that a rule that applies automatically after (37) and after
(39) — hence also to NPs generated in the article position by base
rules — assigns the possessive formative to the final word of the
noun phrase in question.) A similar analysis would hold for derived
nominals, giving such phrases as *(several of) the proofs of the
theorem by John, several proofs of the theorem by John* (which is
nondefinite, as we can see from the sentence *there were several
proofs of the theorem (by John) in the most recent issue of the
journal)*, etc. When the noun phrase constitutes the full determiner

in the surface structure, the feature in question must be interpreted as definite, as we can see from the impossibility of * *there were John's proofs of the theorem in the journal*, with the same interpretation.

Rule (42) is not formulable within the framework that we have so far presupposed (cf. Note 1), which takes feature complexes to be associated only with lexical categories, and permits complex symbols to dominate a sequence of elements only within the word (cf. Chomsky (1965, p. 188f.)). It has been suggested a number of times that this restriction is too heavy and that certain features should also be associated with nonlexical phrase categories.[30] The present considerations lend further support to these proposals.

Such an extension of the theory of syntactic features suggests that the distinction between features and categories is a rather artificial one. In the earliest work in generative grammar it was assumed that the elements of the underlying base grammar are formatives and categories; each category corresponds to a class of strings of formatives. This assumption was carried over from structuralist syntactic theories, which regarded a grammar as a system of classes of elements derived by analytic procedures of segmentation and classification. For reasons discussed in Chomsky (1965, Chapter 2), it was soon found necessary to depart from this assumption in the case of lexical categories. The resulting "mixed theory" had a certain technical artificiality, in that lexical categories were interpreted both as categories of the base (N, V, etc.) and as features in the lexicon ($+ N$, $+ V$, etc.). In fact, when the reliance on analytic

---

[30] See Weinreich (1966), and McCawley (1967). Several of the arguments presented in these papers seem to me very weak, however. For example, McCawley argues that indices must be assigned to full noun phrases rather than to nouns, as suggested in *Aspects*. But this argument follows from an assumption which I see no reason to accept, namely, that in the theory outlined by Chomsky (1965), an index must be assigned to the noun *hat* in such sentences as *John bought a red hat and Bill bought a brown one*. This assumption in turn follows from a theory of indices as referents which I find unintelligible, since it provides no interpretation, so far as I can see, for the case in which nouns are used with no specific intended reference, or for plurals of indefinite or infinite reference, and so on. Until these matters are cleared up, I see no force to McCawley's contention.

procedures of segmentation and classification is abandoned, there is no reason to retain the notion of category at all, even for the base. We might just as well eliminate the distinction of feature and category, and regard all symbols of the grammar as sets of features. If the elements NP, VP, and so on are treated as certain feature complexes, then there is no incoherence in supposing that there are complex symbols of the form [+ def, + NP]. Of course, it is necessary to stipulate with care the precise conditions under which complex symbols can be formed, at each level, or else the system of grammar becomes so powerful as to lose empirical interest. A number of possible restrictions suggest themselves, but I will not explore this general question any further here.

The reanalysis of phrase categories as features permits the formulation of such base rules as (42) as well as the transformational rules that were introduced in our informal discussion of complex noun phrases. It also opens up other possibilities that should be considered. For example, with this reanalysis it becomes possible, under certain restricted circumstances, to introduce new phrase structure through transformations. To illustrate with a concrete example, consider such sentences as (43), (44):

(43)   A man is in the room.

(44)   There is a man in the room.

It is clear, in (44), that *there* is a noun phrase; (44) is subject to such rules, for example, as the interrogative transformation that presupposes this analysis. At the same time, there is some empirical support for the argument that (44) is derived from (43). However, these conclusions are difficult to reconcile within the theory of transformational grammar, since an item (such as *there*) introduced by a transformation can be assigned phrase structure only when it replaces some string which already has this phrase structure; and it requires some artificiality to generate (44) in this way. However, if [+ NP] is a feature (or a complex of features) that can be part of a complex symbol introduced by a transformation, the difficulty is easily removed. For example, if we give to the structure underlying

(43) the proper analysis *(e, e, a man, is, in the room)*[31] and apply the elementary transformation that replaces the first term by the complex symbol [*there*, + NP] *(there* standing for a feature matrix of the usual sort) and the second term by the fourth, which is then deleted, we derive a phrase-marker which is appropriate for further operations.

To take a slightly more complex example, consider such sentences as (45):

(45)   a. What John did was read a book about himself.
        b. What John read was a book about himself.

As noted earlier (p. 39), we might explain some of the properties of these sentences by deriving them from a base structure of roughly the form (46):

(46)

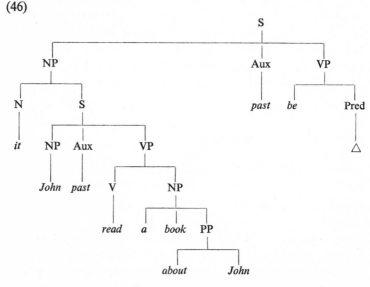

---

[31] Where *e* is the identity element. To be more precise, the structural description of the transformation would have to provide further information, but this goes beyond the detail necessary to clarify the point at issue. One might extend this operation of *there*-insertion, introducing the complex symbol [*there*, + NP, α *plural*] (α = + or α = —), where the third term in the proper analysis (*a man*, in the cited example) is [α *plural*], plurality now being regarded as a

We might then derive (45b) in the following way: Familiar rules apply to the most deeply embedded S to give *John past read a book about himself*. A new substitution transformation replaces the unspecified predicate Δ of (46) by the object of the embedded sentence, *a book about himself*, leaving a "PRO-form" in its place. This gives: *it-John past read it-past be-a book about himself*. Relativization and other familiar rules, supplemented by a rule that replaces *it that* by *what*, give (45b).

But consider now (45a). Again, the most deeply embedded S is converted to *John read a book about himself*. But in this case, the new substitution transformation replaces the unspecified predicate not by the object of the embedded sentence but by its whole verb phrase, which is replaced by a "PRO-form", *do-it*, giving *it-John past do it-past be-read a book about himself*. The remaining rules give (45a). The problem, however, is that the element *do-it* must be specified as a structure of the form V-NP. This is straightforward in the case of the "PRO-verb" *do*, but in the earlier framework there was no way to specify that *it* is a NP in the derived structure. Observe that the embedded VP is replaced by *do-it* even when it contains no NP at all, as in *what John did was read*. The argument that the introduced element *do-it* is actually of the form V-NP is greatly strengthened by other forms, for example, the sentence (47),[32] in which case passivization applies to it:

(47)   John apologized more meekly than it had ever been done before.

Once again, if phrase categories are reinterpreted as features, there is no problem in formulating the required rules. The verb of the embedded VP can become *do* by an extension of the rule of

---

feature that ascends from a head noun to the NP node dominating it. This would make it possible for the rule of *there*-insertion to precede the rule of number agreement. It would also make possible the derivation of *there are believed to be CIA agents in the university* from *it is believed [there to be CIA agents in the university]* just as *CIA agents are believed to be in the university* might derive from *it is believed [CIA agents to be in the university]*, along lines described in Rosenbaum (1967).

[32]   Brought to my attention by John Ross.

do-insertion, and the complex symbol [*it*, + NP] is introduced by the transformation in the appropriate position.

In short, there is some motivation for the limited extension of the mechanisms for assigning derived constituent structure that results from a decision to replace categories systematically by features that can enter into complex symbols.

Continuing to explore consequences of the lexicalist hypothesis, let us return to the rules (21) which expand NP, VP, and AP into expressions containing optional complements. The phrase category "complement" seems to play no role in transformations. We can easily abolish this category if we replace the rules (21) by a single schema, with a variable standing for the lexical categories N, A, V. To introduce a more uniform notation, let us use the symbol $\bar{X}$ for a phrase containing X as its head. Then the base rules introducing N, A, and V will be replaced by a schema (48), where in place of ... there appears the full range of structures that serve as complements and X can be any one of N, A, or V:

(48) $\bar{X} \to X \ldots$

Continuing with the same notation, the phrases immediately dominating $\bar{N}$, $\bar{A}$ and $\bar{V}$ will be designated $\bar{\bar{N}}$, $\bar{\bar{A}}$, $\bar{\bar{V}}$ respectively. To introduce further terminological uniformity, let us refer to the phrase associated with $\bar{N}$, $\bar{A}$, $\bar{V}$ in the base structure as the "specifier" of these elements. Then the elements $\bar{N}$, $\bar{A}$, $\bar{V}$ might themselves be introduced in the base component by the schema (49):

(49) $\bar{\bar{X}} \to [\text{Spec}, \bar{X}] \, \bar{X}$

where [Spec, $\bar{N}$] will be analyzed as the determiner, [Spec, $\bar{V}$] as the auxiliary (perhaps with time adverbials associated), and [Spec, $\bar{A}$] perhaps as the system of qualifying elements associated with adjective phrases (comparative structures, *very*, etc.). The initial rule of the base grammar would then be (50) (with possible optional elements added):

(50) $S \to \bar{\bar{N}} \, \bar{\bar{V}}$.

Thus a skeletal form of the base is induced by the "primitive" categories N, A, V (which, as noted earlier, may themselves be the reflection of an underlying feature structure).

In other respects, the primitive categories might differ, for example, if $\bar{V}$ is analyzed into a copula-predicate construction. Furthermore, it can be expected that the base rules for any language will contain language-specific modifications of the general pattern. If this line of thought is correct, the structure of derived nominals would be something like (51), and the structure of a related sentence, like (52) (omitting much detail):

(51)

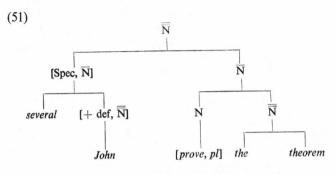

(several of John's proofs of the theorem)

(52)

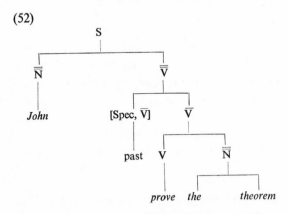

(John proved the theorem)

The internal structure of the nominal (51) mirrors that of the sentence (52). The strict subcategorization features of the lexical item *prove* take account of the phrases $\bar{V}$ and $\bar{N}$ dominating the category to which it is assigned in (51), (52), respectively. Its selectional features refer to the heads of the associated phrases, which are the same in both cases. The category $\bar{\bar{N}}$, like S, is a recursive element of the base.[33] Correspondingly, it would be natural to suppose that in the cyclic application of transformations, the phrases of the form $\bar{\bar{N}}$ play the same role as the phrases of the form S in specifying the domain of transformations.

A structure of the sort just outlined is reminiscent of the system of phrase structure analysis developed by Harris in the 1940's.[34] In Harris' system, statements applying to categories represented in the form X^n (*n* a numeral) applied also to categories represented in the form X^m ($m < n$). One might seek analogous properties of the system just analyzed.

So far, we have surveyed some evidence in support of the lexicalist hypothesis and explored its consequences for grammatical theory and the analysis of English structure. As was noted, the central objection to any form of the lexicalist hypothesis in earlier work such as Lees (1960) was eliminated by later elaborations of syntactic theory to incorporate syntactic features and a separate lexicon. Other objections remain, however. The strongest and most interesting conclusion that follows from the lexicalist hypothesis is that derived nominals should have the form of base sentences, whereas gerundive nominals may in general have the form of transforms. We have indicated that in many cases this conclusion is confirmed, and that at least some apparent counterexamples (e.g., *the city's destruction by the enemy*) can be satisfactorily explained in terms of independently motivated rules. There remain, however, certain more difficult cases. As is well-known, processes

---

[33] The same conclusion is argued on different grounds by Lakoff and Peters (1966). Further evidence that transformations apply to the domain $\bar{\bar{N}}$ is provided by the fact (pointed out to me by John Ross) that extraposition from the determiner takes place inside a noun phrase, as in: *one of the boys who are here who is a friend of mine.*
[34] Harris (1951, Chapter 16).

of derivational morphology are applicable in sequence — they may even be recursive.[35] But consider such expressions as (53):

(53)   a. The book is readable.
           b. the book's readability
           c. John is self-indulgent.
           d. John's self-indulgence

If the lexicalist hypothesis is accepted for the full range of derived nominals, then (53b) and (53d) must be analyzed in terms of base structures such as (51). Since *readability* and *self-indulgence* are obviously derived from *readable* and *self-indulgent*, it follows that (53a) and (53c) must in effect also be base structures rather than transforms from other structures such as, perhaps (54):

(54)   a. the book is able [$_S$for the book to be read]$_S$
           b. John is indulgent to John.

However, a case can be made for transformational derivation of (53a) and (53c) from something like (54a) and (54b), contradicting the lexicalist hypothesis, in this instance.

The seriousness of this objection to the lexicalist hypothesis depends on the strength of the case for the transformational derivation in question. It seems to me that the case is far from persuasive. Notice, for one thing, that the proposed transformation is not "meaning-preserving" (except in the trivialized sense discussed on p. 19), as Chapin observes. In fact, the remarks of Note 10 can be extended to these cases as well. Thus, *readable* is much more sharply restricted in meaning than *able to be read*. In a wide range of other cases the meaning is restricted or based on a very different subregularity (consider *commendable, abominable, irreplaceable, incomparable, despicable, decidable, laudable, insufferable, noticeable, changeable, pitiable, enviable, preferable, insufferable, inviolable, admirable, deplorable, adorable, irritable, lamentable, quotable, detestable, lovable, admissible, livable, laughable, honorable, valuable,*

---

[35] Some examples are discussed by Chapin (1967), which presents the case for the transformationalist hypothesis on the grounds to which we now briefly turn.

and so on).[36] It follows that any argument for the transformational analysis that is based on semantic grounds or on grounds of selectional relations will be very weak.

In fact, even in the best of cases such arguments are weak; correspondingly, since the earliest work in transformational generative grammar, the attempt has been made to support them by independent syntactic arguments. The reason is that an alternative, nontransformational approach can be envisaged if the support for transformations is simply meaning equivalence or sameness of selectional relations. Where the grounds are semantic, an alternative is an enrichment of the rules of semantic interpretation;[37] and regularities involving only selectional features might in principle be stated as redundancy rules of the lexicon.[38] For example, insofar as a subregularity exists regarding selectional rules in the case of *-able*, it can be formulated as a lexical rule that assigns the feature $[X\ -]$ to a lexical item $[V\text{-}able]$ where V has the intrinsic selectional feature $[-\ X]$. It would follow, then, that where the embedded passive in (54a) has as its grammatical subject a noun phrase that is not the underlying object (or, in the case of "pseudo-passives" such as *he can be relied on*, the "pseudo-object"), the corresponding form (53a) will be excluded. In fact, there is evidence in support of this conclusion. Thus we cannot derive *John is*

---

[36] There are also, of course, many cases where there is no possible base form such as (54a), e.g., *probable, feasible, (im)practicable, formidable, peaceable, knowledgeable, perishable, appreciable, sociable, flexible, amiable, variable, actionable, amenable, reasonable, seasonable, personable, miserable, venerable, inexorable, favorable, pleasurable, palatable, tractable, delectable, ineluctable, salable, habitable, creditable, profitable, hospitable, charitable, comfortable, reputable, irascible, incredible, audible, legible, eligible, negligible, intelligible, indelible, horrible, visible, sensible, responsible, accessible, possible, plausible, compatible.*

[37] Such an alternative is of course programmatic insofar as semantic interpretation remains obscure. But the necessity for rules that relate deep structures to (absolute) semantic interpretations seems clear, and it is dangerous to base any argument on the fact that we know little about such rules. If we knew nothing about phonology, it would be tempting to try to account for phonetic form by much more elaborate syntactic processes. Knowing something about phonology, we can see why this step is ill-advised.

[38] As was pointed out to me by E. Klima.

believable (imaginable, expectable, etc.) *to have left* from *NP believes (imagines, expects) John to have left,* although a deep object such as *this claim* can appear in the context — *is believable.* There are many open questions regarding such constructions, but it seems to me that the argument for a transformational analysis of (53a) is not compelling.

What is more, the argument for a transformational analysis of (53b) from (53a) is weak on independent grounds. Thus it is difficult to see how such an analysis could account for the fact that *readability* may refer not to a fact, event, process, etc., but rather to a property; thus the phrase *the readability of the book is its only redeeming feature* does not mean *(the fact) that the book is readable is its only redeeming feature.* Although perhaps such difficulties can be overcome, as matters now stand, examples such as (53a), (53b) do not seem to me to offer a serious argument against the lexicalist hypothesis.

The situation seems to me similar in the case of (53c) and (53d). Examples such as (53c) seem to provide the strongest case for transformational analysis of derived forms, but even here, the matter is far from clear. Consider, for example, the sentences in (55):

(55)   a. John sent a self-addressed envelope.
      b. This is clearly a self-inflicted wound.
      c. The prophecy is self-fulfilling.
      d. Confrontations between students and administration are self-generating.
      e. John is self-educated.
      f. John's remarks are self-congratulatory.
      g. John's actions are self-destructive.

Sentence (55a) does not mean that the envelope was addressed to itself; the phrase *self-addressed envelope* can appear in sentences where there is no syntactic source for *self* at all *(self-addressed envelopes are barred by law from the mails).* The same is true of (55b), (55f), (55g). Sentence (55c) does not, strictly speaking, mean that the prophecy fulfilled the prophecy, which is senseless, but rather that it led to a state of affairs that fulfilled the prophecy. In the case of (55d), what is meant is that certain confrontations generate other confrontations of the same sort; confrontations do not generate themselves. (55e) cannot be derived by a rule analogous to one that purportedly forms (53c) from (54b), since the postulated underlying form, *John was educated by himself*, is ruled out by the principle, whatever it may be, that makes passives incompatible with reflexivization. A similar argument applies to (55g); the postulated underlying form, *John's actions destroy himself*, is ruled out by general conditions on reflexivization. Furthermore, a consideration of forms such as *self-conscious, self-proclaimed (enemy), self-contained, self-evident, self-esteem, self-explanatory* (i.e., needs no explanation), *self-important, self-seeking*, and so on makes one search for a general transformational analysis of such structures seem ill-conceived. The variety and idiosyncrasy of such items seem to be of the sort that is characteristic of the lexicon; it is difficult to see how they can be accounted for by syntactic rules of any generality. Furthermore, the difficulties in deriving (53b) from (53a) carry over to the pair (53c), (53d).

The discussion so far has been restricted to gerundive and derived nominals, and has barely touched on a third category with some peculiar properties, namely, nominals of the sort illustrated in (56):

(56)   a. John's refusing of the offer
        b. John's proving of the theorem
        c. the growing of tomatoes

These forms are curious in a number of respects, and it is not at all clear whether the lexicalist hypothesis can be extended to cover them. That it should be so extended is suggested by the fact that these forms, like derived nominals, appear to have the internal structure of noun phrases; thus the possessive subject can be replaced by a determiner, as in (56c). On the other hand, adjective insertion seems quite unnatural in this construction. In fact, there is an artificiality to the whole construction that makes it quite resistant to systematic investigation. Furthermore, the construction is quite limited. Thus we cannot have *the feeling sad, the trying to win, the arguing about money, the leaving,* etc.

In apparent conflict with an extension of the lexicalist hypothesis is the fact that these constructions exist in the case of certain verbs that we have tentatively derived from underlying intransitives, as in the case of (56c), which is structurally ambiguous, as contrasted with the derived nominal (57), discussed on p. 25, which is unambiguous:

(57)   the growth of tomatoes

If the lexicalist hypothesis is extended to the forms (56), then we must suppose that both *tomatoes grow* and *NP grows tomatoes* are base forms. However, to account for the interpretation of (57) as well as for the relation of transitive and intransitive *grow* we were led to regard *NP grows tomatoes* as the causative of the underlying structure *tomatoes grow*.[39] These various assumptions are mutually consistent only if we reject the analysis of the causative discussed on p. 25, which postulated the base structure (58) for *John grows tomatoes*, and assume instead that the base structure is (59):

(58)   John [+ cause] [$_s$tomatoes grow]$_s$
(59)   John [+ cause, grow] tomatoes

In other words, we postulate that there is a feature [+ cause] which can be assigned to certain verbs as a lexical property. Associated with this feature are certain redundancy rules which are, in this case, universal, hence not part of the grammar of English but rather among the principles by which any grammar is interpreted. These principles specify that an intransitive with the feature [+ cause] becomes transitive and that its selectional features are systematically revised so that the former subject becomes the object. Similar principles of redundancy apply to the associated rules of semantic interpretation. To account for the distinction between

[39] An alternative analysis that derives *tomatoes grow* from *NP grows tomatoes* is implausible, since it would imply that *children grow* derives from * *NP grows children*. See Chomsky (1965, p. 214).

(56c) and (57), we must restrict the feature [+ cause] with respect to the feature that distinguishes derived nominals such as *growth* from forms such as *growing*, limiting it to the latter case. Unless there are some general grounds for the hierarchy thus established, the explanation offered earlier for the nonambiguity of (57) is weakened, since it involves an *ad hoc* step. There is, nevertheless, a partial explanation and a natural way of stating a complex of facts.

To summarize, three types of nominalizations have been considered in this discussion: the gerundive nominals such as (60), the derived nominals such as (61), and the "mixed" forms (62), which to me seem rather clumsy, though quite comprehensible, when a derived nominal also exists:

(60)   John's refusing the offer

(61)   John's refusal of the offer

(62)   John's refusing of the offer

On the basis of the evidence surveyed here, it seems that the transformationalist hypothesis is correct for the gerundive nominals and the lexicalist hypothesis for the derived nominals and perhaps, though much less clearly so, for the mixed forms. This conclusion has a variety of consequences for general linguistic theory and for the analysis of English structure. Such material provides a case study of the complex of problems that arise when linguistic theory is elaborated so as to incorporate both grammatical transformations and lexical features.

REFERENCES

Annear, S., and D. Elliot
   1965   *Derivational Morphology in Generative Grammar.*
Chapin, P.
   1967   "On the Syntax of Word Derivation in English", Ph. D. dissertation, M.I.T.
Hall, B.
   See Partee.

Harris, Z. S.
1951 *Methods in Structural Linguistics*, ch. 16 (Chicago, University of Chicago Press).
Kenny, A.
1963 *Action, Emotion, and Will* (Routledge and Kegan Paul).
Kiparsky, C. and P.
1967 "Fact".
Lakoff, G.
1966 "Some Verbs of Change and Causation".
Lakoff, G., and S. Peters
1966 "Phrasal Conjunction and Symmetric Predicates", Harvard Computation Laboratory, NSF-20.
Langendoen, D. T.
1967 "The Syntax of the English Expletive *it*", *Georgetown University Monographs on Languages and Linguistics* 19 (Washington, D.C.).
Lees, Robert B.
1960 *The Grammar of English Nominalizations* (Mouton).
McCawley, J. D.
1967 "How to find Semantic Universals in the Event that there are Any".
Parttec, Barbara Hall
1965 "Subject and Object in Modern English", Ph. D. Dissertation, M.I.T.
Postal, P.
1966 "Review of R. M. W. Dixon, *Linguistic Science and Logic*", *Language* 42.1, pp. 34-93.
Rosenbaum, P. S.
1967 *The Grammar of English Predicate Complement Constructions* (Cambridge, M.I.T. Press).
Ross, J. R.
1967 "Constraints on variables in syntax", Ph. D. dissertation, M.I.T.
Weinreich, U.
1966 "Explorations in Semantic Theory", in T. A. Sebeok (ed.), *Current Trends in Linguistics*, III (The Hague, Mouton).

DEEP STRUCTURE, SURFACE STRUCTURE
AND SEMANTIC INTERPRETATION*

In a general way, I will be concerned in this paper with the relation
of syntactic structure to semantic representation in generative
grammar. I will outline a general framework within which much of
the discussion of these questions in the past few years can be
reformulated, and alternatives compared as to empirical content
and justification, and I will discuss some empirical considerations
that suggest a choice among these alternatives that is different, in
some respects, from either the theory of grammar outlined in
Chomsky (1965) or the proposals of a more "semantically-based"
grammar that have been developed in the important work of the
past few years. Specifically, these modifications have to do with
some possible contributions of surface structure to delimiting the
meaning of a linguistic expression.

A grammar of a language, in the sense in which I will use this
term, can be loosely described as a system of rules that expresses
the correspondence between sound and meaning in this language.
Let us assume given two universal language-independent systems
of representation, a phonetic system for the specification of sound
and a semantic system for the specification of meaning. As to the
former, there are many concrete proposals; for example, the system
described in detail in chapter 7 of Chomsky and Halle (1968). In the
domain of semantics there are, needless to say, problems of fact
and principle that have barely been approached, and there is no
reasonably concrete or well-defined "theory of semantic representation" to which one can refer. I will, however, assume here that
such a system can be developed, and that it makes sense to speak

* This work was supported in part by the National Institutes of Health
(Grant MH-13390-01).

of the ways in which the inherent meaning of a sentence, characterized in some still-to-be-discovered system of representation, is related to various aspects of its form.

Let us assume further that the grammar in some manner specifies an infinite class of surface structures, each of which is mapped onto a phonetic representation by a system of phonological rules. I assume further that the grammar contains a system of grammatical transformations, each a mapping of phrase-markers onto phrase-markers. In ways that need not concern us in detail, the system of grammatical transformations determines an infinite class K of finite sequences of phrase-markers, each such sequence $P_1, ..., P_n$ meeting the following conditions:

(1)   (i) P_n is a surface structure

(ii) each P_i is formed by applying a certain transformation to P_{i-1} in a way permitted by the conditions on grammatical rules[1]

(iii) there is no P_0 such that $P_0, P_1, ..., P_n$ meets conditions (i) and (ii).

Let us refer to P_1 as a K-INITIAL phrase-marker in this case. We refer to the members of K as the SYNTACTIC STRUCTURES generated by the grammar. So far, we have described K in terms of the class of surface structures, somehow specified, and the system of grammatical transformations, that is, the grammatical transformations of the language and the conditions on how they apply.

[1] Some of the conditions may be specific to the grammar (e.g., certain ordering conditions on transformations), and others general (e.g., the principle of the cycle, in the sense of Chomsky, 1965). These conditions will define certain permissible sequences of transformations and determine how a permissible sequence maps a phrase-marker P onto a phrase-marker P'. Hence with each such permissible sequence $T_1, ..., T_n$ we can associate the class of all sequences of phrase-markers $P_1,..., P_{n+1}$ such that $T_1,..., T_i$ maps P_1 onto P_{i+1} ($1 \leq i \leq n$) in the manner determined. The class K consists of those sequences of phrase-markers which are so associated with permissible sequences of transformations, which terminate with surface structures and which are maximal in the sense of (1iii). Each transformation carries out a certain definite operation on a sub-phrase-marker of the phrase-marker to which it applies; given the principle of the cycle, or others like it, the choice of this sub-phrase-marker may be determined by the position of the transformation in question in the permissible sequence of transformations.

Let us assume further that the grammar contains a lexicon, which we take to be a class of lexical entries each of which specifies the grammatical (i.e., phonological, semantic, and syntactic) properties of some lexical item. The lexicon for English would contain this information for such items as *boy*, *admire*, *tall*, and so on. Just how extensive the lexicon must be — equivalently, just to what extent this information is determined by other parts of the grammar — we leave open. We may think of each lexical entry as incorporating a set of transformations that insert the item in question (that is, the complex of features that constitutes it) in phrase-markers. Thus

(2)   a lexical transformation associated with the lexical item I maps a phrase-marker P containing a substructure Q into a phrase-marker P′ formed by replacing Q by I.

Theories of grammar may differ in the conditions on Q, and more generally, on the nature of these operations.

Suppose, furthermore, that all lexical items are inserted into a phrase-marker before any nonlexical grammatical transformation applies. Thus the grammar meets condition (3):

(3)   Given $(P_1, ..., P_n)$ in K, there is an i such that for $j < i$, the transformation used to form P_{j+1} from P_j is lexical, and for $j \geqslant i$, the transformation used to form P_{j+1} from P_j is nonlexical.[2]

In this case, let us define P_i to be the POST-LEXICAL STRUCTURE of the sequence $P_1, ..., P_n$.

Thus a grammar, so conceived, must have rules specifying the class K and relating each member of K to a phonetic and semantic representation. In particular, the grammar will contain a lexicon and grammatical transformations. Within this general framework, we can describe various approaches to the theory of transfor-

---

[2] In terms of note 1, each permissible sequence of transformations can be analyzed as (L, S) where L is a sequence of lexical transformations and S a sequence of nonlexical (i.e., true syntactic) transformations.

mational-generative grammar that have been explored during the past few years.

The theory outlined in Chomsky (1965) assumes that in addition to a lexicon, a system of grammatical transformations, and a system of phonological rules, the grammar contains a system of rules of semantic interpretation and a context-free categorial component with a designated terminal element Δ. The categorial component and the lexicon are referred to as THE BASE of the grammar. It is assumed that the grammar meets condition (3), so that a class of post-lexical structures is defined. A general well-formedness condition is proposed for surface structures. The class K of syntactic structures consists of those sequences $P_1, ..., P_i, ..., P_n$ (P_1 being the K-initial structure, P_i the post-lexical structure, and P_n the surface structure) meeting condition (1) where, furthermore, P_1 is generated by the categorial component and P_n meets the well-formedness condition for surface structures.[3] Surface structures are mapped into phonetic representations by the phonological rules. Post-lexical structures are mapped into semantic representations by the semantic rules. In this formulation, the post-lexical structures are called DEEP STRUCTURES. The deep structures contain all lexical items, each with its complement of grammatical features. Furthermore, the configurations of the phrase-marker P_1, which are preserved in the deep structure, can be taken to define grammatical relations and functions in a straightforward manner. It is natural (though I shall argue, only in part correct) to suppose that the semantic interpretation of a sentence is determined by the

---

[3] More specifically, a general principle of lexical insertion is formulated which interprets the features (in particular, the contextual features) of lexical entries as lexical insertion transformations and applies these transformations to P_1 giving, ultimately, P_i. A lexical insertion transformation replaces a particular occurrence of the designated symbol Δ of P_1 by a lexical item. Thus in the notation of (2), Q is always Δ and the transformation replaces $Q = \Delta$ by I. We may assume, therefore, that the ordering of $P_1, ..., P_i$ is immaterial—that is, that we consider as syntactic structures equivalence classes defined by the relation among members of K that differ only by a permutation of $P_1, ..., P_i$.

The transformations are said to have a FILTERING FUNCTION in the sense that the well-formedness condition on surface structures must be met.

Several variants of such a theory are discussed in Chomsky (1965).

intrinsic semantic content of lexical items and the manner in which they are related at the level of deep structure. Supposing this (following, in essence, Katz and Postal, 1964), it would follow that deep structures determine semantic representation under the rules of semantic interpretation.

Thus the deep structures, in this theory, are held to meet several conditions. First, they determine semantic representation. Second, they are mapped into well-formed surface structures by grammatical transformations (without any subsequent insertion of lexical items). Third, they satisfy the set of formal conditions defined by base rules; in particular, the rules of the categorial component define the grammatical functions and order of constituents, and the contextual features of lexical entries determine how lexical items can be entered into such structures.

I will refer to any elaboration of this theory of grammar as a "standard theory", merely for convenience of discussion and with no intention of implying that it has some unique conceptual or empirical status. Several such elaborations have been proposed and investigated in the past few years.

Observe that a standard theory specifies, for each sentence, a syntactic structure $\Sigma = (P_1, ..., P_i, ..., P_n)$ (where P_i is the deep and P_n the surface structure), a semantic representation S, and a phonetic representation P. It asserts, furthermore, that S is determined by P_i and P by P_n under the rules of semantic and phonological interpretation, respectively. More generally, the theory is "syntactically-based" in the sense that it assumes the sound-meaning relation (P, S) to be determined by Σ.

It goes without saying that none of the assumptions in the foregoing exposition is self-evident, and that all are open to empirical challenge. Thus, to take perhaps the least controversial, it might be argued that there is no level of phonetic representation, but that syntactic structures are related directly to the organization of peripheral musculature, sensory organs, and neural structures, by operations that are of an entirely different sort than those of grammar. There is no a priori way to demonstrate that this view is incorrect, or to justify the postulation of the level of phonetic representation, which, in this view, is superfluous. The most that one can hope to show is that an interesting range of phenomena can be accounted for by a theory that incorporates a level of phonetic representation of the sort postulated, that there is no crucial counter-evidence, and that there is no reason to suppose that some alternative form of theory will be more successful. Even stronger doubts can be (and often have been) expressed with respect to the notion of semantic representation. Thus one might argue that nonlinguistic beliefs, intentions of the speaker, and other factors enter into the interpretation of utterances in so intimate — and perhaps so fluctuating and indefinite — a fashion that it is hopeless and misguided to attempt to represent independently the "purely grammatical" component of meaning, the various "readings" of expressions in the sense of Katz and Postal (1964) and other versions of the standard theory, and the relation between such readings and a syntactic structure Σ.[4]

[4] The literature relating to this subject is too extensive for detailed reference. See, for example Quine (1960) for discussion of the interpenetration of linguistic and nonlinguistic knowledge. Stampe (1968) argues, in part on grammatical grounds, for a "Gricean view" (see Grice, 1957, 1968) that the notion of "reading" or "semantic interpretation" must be understood in terms of the more basic notion, "Agent-means-x-by-y", an approach which calls into question the possibility of developing a coherent notion of "semantic representation" strictly as part of grammar. For conflicting argument, see Katz (1966), Searle (1968).

There are still other sorts of consideration that might lead one to question the notion of "reading", as construed in recent work. Thus consider such phrases as *John's picture*. In addition to the readings *picture of John* and *picture that John has*, the phrase might be interpreted as *picture that John created, picture that John commissioned*, and no doubt in other ways. On the other hand, *John's puppy* is not subject to the latter two interpretations, though it might mean *puppy to which John (my misnamed pet) gave birth*. On the other hand, it is hardly clear that it is a fact of language that people cannot create (or commission the creation of) puppies in the way in which they can pictures. Correspondingly, it is unclear whether one can assign to these phrases, by rules of grammar, a set of readings that determine how they figure in, say, correct inference. Or consider such a sentence as *I am not against* MY FATHER, *only against* THE LABOR MINISTER, spoken recently by a radical Brazilian student. Knowing further that the speaker is the son of the labor minister, we would assign to this utterance a reading in which the emphasized phrases are coreferential. On one reading, the sentence is contradictory, but knowing the facts just cited a more natural interpretation would be that the speaker is opposed to what his father

If one were to deny the existence of phonetic representation, he might argue that a generative grammar, strictly speaking, is a system of rules relating semantic representation, deep structure, and surface structure, some entirely new sort of theory relating the generated structures to physical signals or perceptual representations. If one were to deny the existence of semantic representation (readings, in the sense of recent discussions), he might argue that a generative grammar is a system of rules relating deep structures, surface structures, and phonetic representation, proposing further that entirely different principles are involved in determining what a person means by saying so-and-so. Evidently, there is no a priori argument against these views, as there is no a priori necessity for a grammar to define systems of deep and surface structure in the sense of the standard theory. Many of the assumptions in the standard theory are uncontroversial in the sense that they have been adopted, explicitly or implicitly, in those studies that attempt to characterize the notion "knowledge of a language", and in that there is no known coherent alternative or any reason, empirical or conceptual, to suppose them inadequate. One should not, however, demand the kind of justification that in principle can never be provided.

In summary, I have so far outlined a certain general framework and a "standard theory" that develops this framework in a specific direction. Furthermore, the literature contains further elaborations of this standard theory, and many realizations of it with respect to particular languages (that is, fragments of grammars of specific languages constructed in terms of the standard theory). At each level, there are reasonable doubts that can be raised, and alternatives can be envisaged. It goes without saying that the investigation of these doubts and the study of alternatives can only be beneficial, in the long run, and should be actively pursued. It must also be

---

does in his capacity as labor minister, and would be accurately paraphrased in this more elaborate way. It is hardly obvious that what we "read into" sentences in such ways as these—no doubt, in a fairly systematic way—can either be sharply dissociated from grammatically determined readings, on the one hand, or from considerations of fact and belief, on the other.

kept in mind that at each level of discussion, justification can only go so far — in particular, that it can never be conclusive.

Given alternative formulations of a theory of grammar, one must first seek to determine how they differ in empirical consequences, and then try to find ways to compare them in the area of difference. It is easy to be misled into assuming that differently formulated theories actually do differ in empirical consequences, when in fact they are intertranslatable — in a sense, mere notational variants. Suppose, for example, that one were to modify the standard theory, replacing condition (3) by the condition that lexical items are inserted just prior to a transformation affecting the configuration in which they appear. Making this notion precise, we could devise an apparent alternative to the standard theory which, however, does not differ at all in empirical consequences, although the notion "deep structure" is not defined, at least in anything like the sense above.[5] Given the central character of this notion in the standard theory, the alternative would appear to be significantly different, though in fact it would be only a notational variant. There would be, in other words, no empirical issue as to which formulation is correct or preferable on empirical grounds. Before the standard theory can be compared with this modification, it is necessary to formulate both in such a way that there is an empirical distinction between them.

Similarly, suppose that one were to counterpose to the "syntactically-based" standard theory a "semantically-based" theory of the following sort. Whereas the standard theory supposes that a syntactic structure Σ is mapped onto the pair (P, S) (P a phonetic and S a semantic representation), the new theory supposes that S is mapped onto Σ, which is then mapped onto P as in the standard theory. Clearly, when the matter is formulated in this way,[6] there

---

[5] We might assume that rules of semantic interpretation of the type proposed by Katz in many publications apply cyclically, in parallel with the rules of the cycle of syntactic transformations, assigning readings to successively "higher" nodes in the process. Thus semantic interpretation would, in effect, match that of the standard theory, though the notion of "deep structure" is not defined.

[6] As, for example, in Chafe (1967). Chafe also proposes to obliterate the

is no empirical difference between the "syntactically-based" standard theory and the "semantically-based" alternative. The standard theory generates quadruples (P, s, d, S) (P a phonetic representation, s a surface structure, d a deep structure, S a semantic representation). It is meaningless to ask whether it does so by "first" generating d, then mapping it onto S (on one side) and onto s and then P (on the other); or whether it "first" generates S (selecting it, however one wishes, from the universal set of semantic representations), and then maps it onto d, then s, then P; or, for that matter, whether it "first" selects the pair (P, d), which is then mapped onto the pair (s, S); etc. At this level of discussion, all of these alternatives are equivalent ways of talking about the same theory. There is no general notion "direction of a mapping" or "order of steps of generation" to which one can appeal in attempting to differentiate the "syntactically-based" standard theory from the "semantically-based" alternative, or either from the "alternative view" which regards the pairing of surface structure and semantic interpretation as determined by the "independently selected" pairing of phonetic representation and deep structure, etc. Before one can seek to determine whether grammar is "syntactically-based" or "semantically-based" (or whether it is based on "independent choice" of paired phonetic representation and deep structure, etc.), one must first demonstrate that the alternatives are genuine and not merely variant ways of speaking in a loose and informal manner about the same system of grammar. This is not so easy or obvious a matter as is sometimes supposed in recent discussion.

Perhaps the point can be clarified by reference to a discussion of Katz and Postal (1964, § 5.4). Katz and Postal develop a variant of what I have called the standard theory, and then discuss how a model of speech production might be envisioned that incorporates a grammar of this sort. They outline a hypothetical procedure as follows: select a "message" which is a set of readings, i.e., of semantic representations in the sense discussed above. Select a

---

distinction between syntax and semantics, but this, too, is merely a terminological issue, as he formulates it.

syntactic structure Σ (in particular, what we have here called the deep structure d in Σ) such that Σ maps onto s by the rules of semantic interpretation of the grammar. However this selection is accomplished, we may regard it as defining a mapping of s onto Σ, and in general, of semantic interpretations onto syntactic structures. Then, map Σ onto a speech signal, making use of the rules of phonological interpretation (giving the phonetic representation P) and rules that relate the latter to a signal. Quite properly, Katz and Postal present this schematic description as an account of a hypothetical PERFORMANCE model. In such a model, it makes sense to speak of order of selection of structures, direction of a mapping, and so on. Suppose, however, that we were to interpret this account as an intuitive instruction for using the rules of the grammar to form quadruples (P, s, d, S), i.e., for generating structural descriptions of sentences. Of course, in this case, the notion of "order of selection of structures" or "intrinsic direction of a mapping" would have no more than an intuitive, suggestive role; the informal instruction would be one of any number of equivalent instructions for using the rules of the grammar to form structural descriptions. To confuse the two kinds of account would be a category mistake. In short, it is necessary to observe the difference in logical character between performance and competence.

Suppose that we were to develop a modification of the standard theory along the following lines. Using the notation presented earlier the standard theory generates syntactic structures $\Sigma = (P_1, ..., P_i, ..., P_n)$, where P_1 is a K-initial, P_i a deep, and P_n a surface structure, P_1 being generated by the categorial component, and P_i formed by lexical insertion transformations that replace the substructure Q of P_1 by a lexical item, Q always being the designated symbol Δ. P_i is then mapped onto a semantic representation S. Suppose further that we regard S as itself a phrase-marker in some "semantically primitive" notation. For example, we may think of the lexical entry for "kill" as specifying somehow a phrase-marker *cause-to-die* that might be related to the phrase-marker that serves as the semantic representation of the phrase "cause to die."[7] Suppose now that in forming Σ, we construct P_1 which is, in fact, the semantic representation of the sentence, and then form $P_2,\ldots, P_i$ by rules of lexical insertion, replacing a substructure Q which is the semantic representation of a lexical item I by I. For example, if P_1 contains $Q = cause\text{-}to\text{-}die$, the lexical entry for "kill" will permit Q to be replaced by $I = $ "kill". Similarly, the lexical entry for "murder" might indicate that it can be inserted by a lexical transformation for the substructure $Q = cause\text{-}to\text{-}die\text{-}by\text{-}unlawful\text{-}means\text{-}and\text{-}with\text{-}malice\text{-}aforethought$, where the grammatical object is furthermore human; and the entry for *assassinate* might specify further that the object is characterized, elsewhere in the phrase-marker, as a reasonably important person; etc. Similarly, the lexical entry for "uncle" might specify that it can replace $Q = brother\ of\ (father\text{-}or\text{-}mother)$. And so on, in other cases.[8]

Superficially, this new theory seems significantly different from the standard theory. Thus deep structures are not mapped into semantic representations in the same sense as in the standard theory; rather the converse is true. Furthermore, the rules of lexical insertion operate in a rather different manner, replacing substructures Q, which may be quite complex, by lexical items.

---

[7] The relation could not be identity, however. As has often been remarked, "causative" verbs such as *kill, raise, burn* (as in *John burned the toast*), etc., differ in meaning from the associated phrases *cause to die, cause to rise, cause to burn*, etc., in that they imply a directness of connection between the agent and the resulting event that is lacking in the latter case. Thus John's negligence can cause the toast to burn, but it cannot burn the toast. Similarly, I can cause someone to die by arranging for him to drive cross-country with a pathological murderer, but I could not properly be said to have killed him, in this case. The point is discussed in Hall (1965).

[8] Systems of this sort have been developed by McCawley in a number of interesting papers (see bibliography). The specific realizations of such systems proposed by McCawley are genuinely different, on empirical grounds, from the specific realizations of the standard theory that have been proposed for English. However, two questions can be raised: first, are the SYSTEMS genuinely different, or are the genuine differences only in the realizations, which could, therefore, be translated into the other general systems of grammar; are the realizations suggested better or worse than the alternatives, on empirical grounds? I will return briefly to the former question, in a specific case.

We might ask, in such a theory, whether there is any natural break between "syntax" and "semantics". We might, in fact, define certain nonlexical transformations that apply in forming the sequence $(P_1, ..., P_i)$, thus violating condition (3) and eliminating the notion "post-lexical structure", hence "deep structure", as defined earlier. Nevertheless, as I have so far formulated the alternatives, it is not at all clear that they are genuine alternatives. It must be determined whether the interpolated "non-lexical" transformations are other than inverses of rules of semantic interpretation, in the standard theory. Furthermore, it is unclear what difference there may be, on empirical grounds, between the two formulations of rules of lexical insertion. Again, before inquiring into the relative merit of alternative systems of grammar, it is necessary to determine in what ways they are empirically distinguishable. To establish that the systems are genuine alternatives, one would have to show, for example, that there is a difference between formulating the lexical insertion operations so that they insert *uncle* in place of the structure Q $=$ *brother of (father-or-mother)* (the terms of Q being "semantically primitive"), on the one hand, and on the other hand, formulating the rules of semantic interpretation so that they assign to "uncle" a position in the space of concepts (represented in terms of "semantic primitives") which is the same as that assigned, by rules of composition of the sort that Katz has discussed, to the phrase "brother of (father-or-mother)". If such a difference can be established, the theories might then be compared, in various ways. For example, one might compare the way in which such related concepts as "kill", "murder", "assassinate" are treated in the two systems, or one might inquire into the nature and generality of the various rules and principles that are presupposed. In general, one might try to show that certain phenomena are explicable in a general way in one system but not in the other. Again, this is not so simple a matter as is sometimes supposed, to judge by recent discussion.

Consider next the following modification of the standard theory. We consider a new set of structures C (for "case systems") which represent semantically significant relations among phrases such as the relation of agent-action in (4) and of instrument-action as in (5):

(4)   John opened the door

(5)   the key opened the door

Suppose we were to assume, in a realization of the standard theory, that the deep structures of (4) and (5) are identical except for lexical entries. Then these deep structures, it might be argued, do not represent the required relations. For example, as grammatical relations are defined in Chomsky (1965), the subject-predicate relation is the relation that holds between *John* and *opened the door* in (4) and between *the key* and *opened the door* in (5); hence the relations of agent-action and instrument-action are not differentiated. Let us therefore construct the structures C_1 and C_2 of C as follows:

(6) C_1: ([V, *open*], [Agent, *John*], [Object, *the door*])

(7) C_2: ([V, *open*], [Instrument, *the key*], [Object, *the door*])

Suppose that the grammar contains a component that generates such structures as C_1 and C_2 and rules that map these onto phrase-markers; for example, the main rule might say that the item specified as Agent takes the position of subject (in the sense of the standard theory), and if there is no Agent, this position is occupied by the Instrument, etc. Formalizing these ideas, we might develop a theory in which C is mapped onto a class of phrase-markers which are K-initial in the sense described earlier, further operations being as the standard theory. However, we drop condition (3) and relate the lexicon and the rules of semantic interpretation directly to C.[9]

---

[9]   Case systems of this sort are developed in an important paper by Charles Fillmore (1968). As in the case of notes 7 and 8, we may ask (i) whether case systems are genuinely distinct from the standard system, or intertranslatable with it; (ii) whether the specific realizations proposed by Fillmore differ empirically from the specific realizations that have been proposed for the standard system; (iii) if so, how do they compare on empirical grounds? As to the second question, the answer is surely positive. Thus Fillmore's specific pro-

Are case systems, so described, empirically distinguishable from the standard system? It is not at all obvious. Thus consider the example just given. It was argued that if (4) and (5) have the same deep structure, apart from lexical entries (let us put aside the question whether this is correct), then the relations indicated in (6) and (7) are not represented in these deep structures. However, this argument depends on an assumption, which need not be accepted, regarding rules of semantic interpretation. In fact, the rules mapping C_1 and C_2 onto the deep structures of (4) and (5), respectively, can be interpreted as rules of semantic interpretation for these deep structures. Thus one rule (probably universal) will stipulate that for verbs of action, the animate subject may be interpreted as the agent; etc. Various qualifications are needed whether we interpret these rules as rules of semantic interpretation or as rules mapping C onto S; I see very little difference between them, at this level of discussion, and the same seems to me true in many more complex cases. It might be argued that the case system expresses these facts in a "direct way" whereas the standard system does so only "indirectly".[10] The distinction seems to me meaningless. Without principles of interpretation, a formal system expresses nothing at all. What it expresses, what information it provides, is determined by these principles.

A good part of the critique and elaboration of the standard theory in the past few years has focussed on the notion of deep structure and the relation of semantic representation to syntactic structure. This is quite natural. No area of linguistic theory is more

---

posals do not permit any transformation (e.g., question or relative formation) to apply prior to such transformations as passive, indirect-object-inversion, and others that have been proposed in standard transformational grammars, and there are other specific differences. A serious discussion of question (iii) would take us too far afield. As Fillmore develops these systems, rules of semantic interpretation relate directly both to C and to the K-initial structures onto which elements of C are mapped, since this operation is not "meaning preserving", in the sense that sentences derived from the same element $c \varepsilon C$ may, as Fillmore observes, differ in meaning.

[10] Similar arguments, equally specious, have been given in support of the view that grammatical relations must be "directly represented" in underlying structures.

veiled in obscurity and confusion, and it may be that fundamentally new ideas and insights will be needed for substantial progress to be made in bringing some order to this domain. I want to investigate one kind of revision of the standard theory that bears directly on the relation of syntax and semantics, but before doing so, I would like to consider briefly one kind of critique of the standard theory — specifically, concerning the status of deep structure — that seems to me to have been, so far, without consequence, though the general approach is quite legitimate and perhaps hopeful. I have in mind a critique analogous to that developed by Halle and others against the concept of the phoneme, a number of years ago. Halle argued that a generative grammar could provide a level of phonemic representation, in the sense of structural linguistics, only by abandoning otherwise valid generalizations. Analogously, one might ask whether the requirement that deep structures exist in the sense of the standard theory (see p. 65, above) is compatible with otherwise valid generalizations. A negative answer would be highly interesting, and the matter therefore deserves serious investigation. A number of papers have dealt with this matter, but, I think, so far unsuccessfully.

McCawley purports to present such an argument in McCawley (in press, postscript).[11] He considers the following expressions:

[11]   I omit here certain aspects of McCawley's argument that seem to me to impose serious difficulties of interpretation. Not the least of these difficulties is the theory of referential indices that McCawley proposes. To mention just the most serious problem, the idea that every noun phrase must have an intended reference, somehow specified in the underlying structure, seems unreconcilable with the fact that I may perfectly well use noun phrases where I know that there is no reference at all and hence intend no reference (e.g., *if you are looking for the fountain of youth, you won't find it here, he is looking for a man who is taller than himself*, etc.). The idea of trying to incorporate "intended reference" in syntax seems to me misguided. It may clarify matters to point out that in Chomsky (1965), to which McCawley refers in this connection, it is not proposed that reference (actual or intended) be incorporated into syntax, but rather that "referential expressions" be indexed in a way relevant to the operation of certain syntactic rules, and that the rules that assign semantic interpretation to syntactic structures refer to identity of indices in determining sameness of intended reference. This may or may not be a useful idea, but it is very different from McCawley's proposal that the intended reference of a noun phrase be

(8)   Ax:xε (John, Harry) [x loves x's wife]
(9)   John loves John's wife and Harry loves Harry's wife
(10)   John and Harry love John's wife and Harry's wife, respectively
(11)   John and Harry love their respective wives
(12)   Ax:xεM [x loves x's wife]
(13)   these men love their respective wives
(14)   that man (x) loves Mary and that man (y) loves Alice
(15)   that man (x) and that man (y) love Mary and Alice respectively
(16)   those men love Mary and Alice respectively

He proposes that (8) and (12) be taken as (approximately) the semantic interpretations of (11) and (13) respectively (where A is the universal quantifier and M is the class of these men). He states further that the transformation which produces (10)[12] is "involved in" the derivation of (11). This transformation, the "*respectively*-transformation", relates (8) to (11), relates (12) to (13), and relates (14) to (16). McCawley furthermore rejects the idea of regarding such sentences as (13) as derived from conjunctions — quite properly: if for no other reason, consider what this proposal would entail for "the real numbers are smaller than their respective squares". Furthermore, (16) "arise[s] from [our (14)] by the *respectively*-transformation", which also maps (17) into (18):

(17)   that man (x) loves Mary and that man (x) loves Alice
(18)   that man (x) and that man (x) love Mary and Alice, respectively

The rule of noun phrase collapsing maps (15) into (16) and (18) into (19):

(19)   that man loves Mary and Alice

---

specified in the grammar by an index, or in his terms, that the index "be" the intended reference.
[12] That is, the "transformation which produces the sentence (145): *John and Harry love Mary and Alice respectively*", which differs from (10) in deep structure, according to him, only in that where (10) has *John's wife* and *Harry's wife*, (145) has *Mary* and *Alice*

Presumably, then, McCawley intends that the respectively-transformation, which is "involved in" the derivation of (11) from (8), in fact maps (9) into (10) exactly as it maps (14) into (15) and (17) into (18). Combining these various comments, McCawley seems to have in mind the following organization of operations:

$$
\begin{array}{cccc}
 & \text{I} & \text{R} & \text{R}' \\
(20) & (8) \rightarrow & (9) \rightarrow & (10) \rightarrow (11) \\
 & \text{I}' & & \\
 & (12) \rightarrow (13) & & \\
 & \text{R} & \text{C} & \\
 & (14) \rightarrow & (15) \rightarrow & (16) \\
 & \text{R} & \text{C} & \\
 & (17) \rightarrow & (18) \rightarrow & (19),
\end{array}
$$

where I and I' are two rules, apparently entirely distinct, relating expressions with quantifiers to phrase-markers of the usual sort; R is a transformation forming sentences with *respectively*; R' is a subsequent transformation that forms noun phrases with *respective*; and C is the rule of noun phrase collapsing.

Having presented this material, McCawley argues as follows. In a standard theory the relation of (8) to (11) and the relation of (12) to (13) must be regarded as semantic (since it involves "a relationship between a representation involving quantifiers and bound variables and a representation involving ordinary noun phrases"), whereas the relation between (14) and (16) (or (17) and (19)) is syntactic, namely, it is expressed by the transformation of conjunction-reduction. McCawley then concludes, without further argument, "that *respectively* can not be treated as a unitary phenomenon in a grammar with a level of deep structure and that that conception of grammar must be rejected" in favor of a "semantically-based" theory. This argument is held to be analogous to Halle's argument against the level of phonemic representation.

Even if we accept McCawley's analysis *in toto*, no conclusion follows with respect to the concept of deep structure. His argument is based on an equivocation in the use of the notion "*respectively*-transformation", and collapses when the equivocation is removed.

Thus if we use the term "*respectively*-transformation" to refer to the relation of (8) to (11), (12) to (13), (14) to (16), and (17) to (19), then this "transformation" does, as he says, relate semantic to syntactic representations in the first two cases, and syntactic representations to syntactic representations in the latter two. But in the analysis he proposes, namely (20), the "*respectively*-transformation" carries out four totally different operations; hence it does not express a "unitary phenomenon". If, on the other hand, we use the term "*respectively*-transformation" to denote R of (20), then it does express a "unitary phenomenon", but it no longer relates semantic to syntactic representation in one case and syntactic to syntactic representation in the other. In fact, (20) can be formulated in the standard theory, if we take I and I' to be inverses of rules of semantic interpretation, and R, R' and C to be syntactic transformations. Therefore McCawley's analysis, right or wrong, is simply a realization of the standard theory, once equivocations of terminology are removed. Consequently, it shows nothing about the level of deep structure. Furthermore, it does not treat the phenomena in question in a "unitary" manner, since no relation is proposed between I and I'.[13]

I have analyzed McCawley's argument in some detail, both because it is now often referred to as demonstrating the impossibility of incorporating the concept of deep structure in a generative grammar, and because this analysis illustrates clearly some of the difficulties in constructing a genuine alternative to the standard theory.

McCawley observes, quite correctly, that it is necessary to provide some justification for the hypothesis of an "intermediate" level of deep structure: "there is no a priori reason why a grammar could not instead[14] consist of 'say' a 'formation rule' component which

---

[13] A very different interpretation of these phenomena, in a somewhat-modified version of the standard theory, is presented in Dougherty (1968a). Dougherty's version of the standard theory is close enough to it so that his analysis can be compared on empirical grounds with McCawley's, which is, so far as I can see, entirely within the standard theory (if we drop the matter of indices as intended referents).

[14] The word *instead*, however, begs a number of questions, for reasons already

specifies the membership of a class of well-formed semantic representations, and a 'transformational component' which consists of rules correlating semantic representations with surface syntactic representation...". The same might be said about "surface structure", "semantic representation" and "phonetic representation". There is only one way to provide some justification for a concept that is defined in terms of some general theory, namely, to show that the theory provides revealing explanations for an interesting range of phenomena and that the concept in question plays a role in these explanations. In this sense, each of the four concepts just mentioned, along with the notion of grammatical transformation and a number of others, receives some justification from the linguistic work that is based on grammars of the standard form. Of course, there is no a priori reason why the standard theory should be correct, so far as it goes in specifying the form of grammar; in fact, I will argue later that it is not. I fail to see what more can be said, at the level of generality at which McCawley develops his critique.

Lakoff has approached the same question — namely, whether deep structures can be defined in the sense of the standard theory without loss of significant generalization — in a more tentative way, in an interesting paper on instrumental adverbs (Lakoff, 1968). He considers such sentences as (21) and (22)

---

noted. Thus in describing the standard theory one might refer to the deep structures as "well-formed semantic representations", associating each with the class of readings into which it can be mapped by rules of semantic interpretation. Similarly, one might regard McCawley's "semantic representations", which, he proposes, be represented as phrase-markers, as nothing other than the deep structures of the standard theory, the "formation rules" being the rules of the categorial component that form K-initial structures and the lexical rules that form deep structures from them by lexical insertion. McCawley in fact assumes that mutually deducible sentences may have different "semantic representations" (in his sense), these being related by "logic", a concept not further specified. To formulate his proposal in the standard theory, we might then take "logic" to incorporate the rules of semantic interpretation (which express the "logic of concepts", in one traditional use of this term). In this respect too he fails to differentiate his theory from the standard theory. McCawley discusses some of these questions in (1968a), but inconclusively, I think, in part for reasons mentioned above on p. 72-73.

(21)   Seymour sliced the salami with a knife
(22)   Seymour used a knife to slice the salami

and gives a number of arguments to show that despite differences of surface structure, the same grammatical and selectional relations appear in these sentences. He argues that the two must have the same, or virtually the same representations in deep structure if selectional features and grammatical relations are to be statable in terms of deep structures, in anything like the sense of the standard theory. He suggests at various points that (22) is much closer to this common deep structure than (21); consequently, instrumental adverbs do not appear in deep structure, and the grammatical relations and selectional features must be associated, for both (21) and (22), with deep structures of roughly the form (22'):

(22')

$$
\begin{array}{ccccccc}
\text{NP} & \text{V} & \text{NP} & [_\text{S} & \text{NP} & \text{V} & \text{NP} \quad]_\text{S} \\
| & | & \wedge & & | & | & \wedge \\
\text{Seymour} & \text{used} & \text{a knife} & & \text{Seymour} & \text{sliced} & \text{the salami}
\end{array}
$$

Alternatively, the concept of deep structure, in the sense of the standard theory, must be abandoned.

Lakoff's argument is indirect; he does not propose underlying structures or grammatical rules, but argues that whatever they are, they must meet a variety of conditions in an adequate grammar, these conditions suggesting either a deep structure such as (22') or the abandonment of the notion deep structure. He points out that if (22') underlies (21), deep structures must be quite abstract, since (21), which contains only one verb, is based on a structure with an embedded sentence and hence with two verbs. In either case, it would be fair to conclude that a departure from the standard theory is indicated.[15]

---

[15]   In the case of the double verb, what is a departure from more familiar formulations is that in this proposal, the verb *slice* in an embedded underlying sentence becomes the main verb, and the main verb *use* is deleted. On the other hand, it has been suggested many times, in realizations of the standard theory, that items that are in some sense relatively "empty" of semantic content (such as *be, have. use,* etc.) may be deleted from embedded sentences.

However, the argument is weakened — I think, vitiated — by the fact that a number of structures are omitted from consideration that seem highly relevant to the whole matter.[16] Thus alongside of (21) and (22), we have such sentences as (23)-(26):

(23)   Seymour used the knife to slice the salami with
(24)   Seymour used this table to lean the ladder against
(25)   Seymour used this table to write the letter on
(26)   Seymour used this car to escape (make his getaway) in

Such facts as these suggest that underlying (22) is a structure such as (27):

(27)   Seymour used a knife [$_S$Seymour sliced the salami with a knife]$_S$

Seymour used this table [$_S$Seymour leaned the ladder against this table]$_S$

---

[16]   There are also quite a number of relevant factual questions that might be raised. Thus Lakoff assumes that (21) and (22) are synonymous. This is not obvious; compare *John carelessly broke the window with a hammer, John broke the window carelessly with a hammer, John carelessly used a hammer to break the window, John used the hammer carelessly to break the window.* The differences of meaning suggest a difference in the meaning of the sentences from which the adverb is omitted. Similarly, consider the many sentences in which *use* and *to* have the sense appropriate to this discussion, but which do not correspond to sentences with instrumental adverbs: e.g., *John used his connections to further his career, John used the classroom to propagandize for his favorite doctrines, John used the mallet over and over again to reduce the statue to rubble.* Or consider such sentences as (A): *John used this hammer and that chisel to sculpt the figure.* Believing (A), one would be entitled to give a positive answer to the question *did John use that chisel to sculpt the figure?* but not to: *did John sculpt the figure with that chisel?* The matter is even clearer if we consider *John used this hammer and that chisel in sculpting the figure,* which Lakoff considers synonymous with (A) — see p. 12 of his paper.

See Bresnan (1968), for other relevant arguments.

A full analysis would have to bring much other evidence to bear — e.g., such sentences as *Seymour sliced the salami without (using) a knife,* which are not paired with anything like (22), and which suggest that insofar as the deep structures are common, it may be that *use* is embedded below *slice* in (21), rather than conversely, as Lakoff suggests.

I do not see how these questions can be resolved without undertaking an analysis of these structures which does propose rules as well as underlying structures, and in this sense, goes well beyond the approach to these questions that Lakoff presents.

The latter might then be compared with such sentences as *Seymour used the knife for a strange purpose, ... in a strange way*, etc. To form (23)-(26), a deletion operation will delete the final NP in the embedded sentence of (27) (an operation analogous, perhaps, to the one used in deriving *meat is good to eat*). The preposition *with*, furthermore, can optionally be deleted, giving (21) from (23). In (24), *against* cannot be deleted, but the corresponding preposi- tions can optionally be deleted (in some styles at least) in (25) and (26), giving (28) and (29) which do not correspond at all to (30) and (31), respectively:

(28) Seymour used this table to write the letter, this is the table that Kant used to write the *Critique*, etc.
(29) Seymour used this car to escape (make his getaway)
(30) Seymour wrote the letter with this table
(31) Seymour escaped (made his getaway) with this car [rather, "in this car"]

Very likely, a still more satisfactory analysis can be given, taking other data into account — see note 16. However, the relevant point here is that a wider range of data than Lakoff considered suggests an underlying structure such as (27) for (22); and if this is the case, then the major problems that Lakoff raises dissolve, as can be seen by checking case by case.[17] In particular, deep structures

[17] In some cases, an explanation can be suggested for facts that would require arbitrary stipulation were the underlying structure to be taken as (22′) — e.g., the fact that the complement of *use* may not contain an instrumental adverb — see p. 21 of Lakoff, *op. cit.* Many of the interesting phenomena that Lakoff notes still demand explanation, of course, but this fact does not help choose among the alternatives, since no explanation or even satisfactory descriptive account is offered in either case.

It is perhaps worth mentioning that the rather similar analysis of manner adverbials presented in Lakoff (1965) is also quite unpersuasive on factual grounds. Lakoff argues that the manner adverbials too are derived from "higher predicates", with sentence (i), for example, serving as an approximate source of (ii):

(i) John is reckless in hanging from trees
(ii) John hangs from trees recklessly

However, (i) is clearly ambiguous, having either the approximate sense (α) or (β):

(α) John is reckless in that he hangs from trees

for (21) and (22), though not identical in this analysis, would nevertheless express the required selectional and grammatical relations in a unified way. And none of Lakoff's general conclusions with regard to deep structure follow if this analysis, or something like it, is correct.

Turning to a somewhat different matter, let us consider once again the problem of constructing a "semantically-based" theory of generative grammar that is a genuine alternative to the standard theory. Reviewing the observations made earlier, the standard theory has the general structure indicated in (32), where P_1 is the K-initial phrase-marker, P_i the deep structure, and P_n the surface structure of $\Sigma \varepsilon K$, and where P is a phonetic and S a semantic representation:

$$(32) \quad \Sigma = (P_1, ..., P_i, ..., P_n)$$

$$S \qquad P$$

S is determined from P_i by rules of semantic interpretation, and P from P_n by phonological rules. Only operations of lexical insertion apply prior to P_i, and none apply subsequently; P_1 is generated

---

(β) John is reckless in the way he hangs from trees

Sentence (ii) has only the interpretation (β). But (β) itself no doubt derives from something of the form (γ), in which the embedded sentence would be something like (δ), which contains a manner adverbial—in place of *in that way* one might have *in a reckless way, in a way that is reckless, recklessly.*

    (γ)   John is reckless in the way in which he hangs from trees

    (δ)   John hangs from trees in that way

Hence it appears that rather than (i) underlying (ii), it is more likely that something like (α) and (γ) underlie (i) and only (γ) underlies (ii), where (γ) contains an embedded structure like (δ) with an inherent manner adverbial.

Notice that in (iii) and (iv) the interpretation is along the lines of (α), in (v) it is along the lines of (β), and in (vi) it is ambiguous as between (α) and (β):

    (iii)   clumsily, John trod on the snail

    (iv)   John trod on the snail, clumsily

    (v)   John trod on the snail clumsily

    (vi)   John clumsily trod on the snail.

The examples are discussed in Austin (1956-7). Such sentences as *John stupidly stayed in England* are unambiguously interpreted along the lines of (α), and, correspondingly, the analogue to (v) is ungrammatical. These facts can be accommodated by an approach that takes (α) and (γ) as approximating the underlying sources, but they do not appear consistent with Lakoff's analysis.

by the categorial component of the base. Each element of Σ is formed from the preceding one by a transformation, the exact effect of each transformation being determined, by general conditions, by the position of this operation in the sequence of transformational operations that generates Σ. The grammar generates quadruples (S, P_i, P_n, P). As emphasized earlier, there is no precise sense to the question: which of these is selected "first" and what is the "direction" of the relations among these formal objects. Consequently, it is senseless to propose as an alternative to (32) a "semantically-based" conception of grammar in which S is "selected first" and then mapped onto the surface structure P_n and ultimately P.

Consider once again a theory such as that proposed by McCawley in which P_1 is identified with S and condition (3) is dropped so that "deep structure" is undefined. Let us consider again how we might proceed to differentiate this formulation — let us call it "semantically-based grammar" — from the standard theory. Consider such expressions as (33)-(35):

(33)   John's uncle
(34)   the person who is the brother of John's mother or father or the husband of the sister of John's mother or father
(35)   the person who is the son of one of John's grandparents or the husband of a daughter of one of John's grandparents, but is not his father

If the concept "semantic representation" ("reading") is to play any role at all in linguistic theory, then these three expressions must have the same semantic representation. But now consider the context (36):

(36)   Bill realized that the bank robber was —

and the sentences S_{33}, S_{34}, S_{35} formed by inserting (33), (34), (35), respectively, in (36). Evidently, the three sentences S_{33}, S_{34}, S_{35} are not paraphrases; it is easy to imagine conditions in which each might be true and the other two false. Hence if the concept "semantic representation" (or "reading") is to play any serious role in linguistic theory, the sentences S_{33}, S_{34}, S_{35}, must have different semantic representations (readings). Many such examples can be constructed. The basic point is that what one believes, realizes, etc.,[18] depends not only on the proposition expressed, but also on some aspects of the form in which it is expressed. In particular, then, people can perfectly well have contradictory beliefs, can correctly be said to fail to realize that p even though (in another sense) they know that p, to be aware that p but be unaware that q where p and q are different expressions of the same proposition, etc. Notice that there is nothing in the least paradoxical about these observations. It is the function of such words as *realize*, *be aware of*, etc. to deal with such situations as those just described, which are perfectly common and quite intelligible.

Given these observations, let us return to the standard and semantically-based theories. In the standard theory, (33), (34), and (35) would derive from three different deep structures, all mapped onto the same semantic representation. To assign a different meaning to S_{33}, S_{34} S_{35}, it is necessary to define *realize* (i.e., assign it intrinsic lexical semantic properties) in such a way that the meaning assigned to "NP realizes that p" depends not only on the semantic interpretation of p but also on the deep structure of p. In the case in question, at least, there is no contradiction in this requirement, though it remains to meet it in an interesting way.

In the case of the semantically-based theory this alternative is of course ruled out. In fact, within the framework of this theory it is impossible to accept all of the following conditions on K-initial structures (semantic representations, in this formulation):

(37)   At the level of K-initial structures:

        (i) (33), (34), (35) have the same representation

       (ii) S_{33}, S_{34}, S_{35} have different representations

      (iii) the representation of (36) is independent of which

---

[18] Similarly, what one can prove, demonstrate, etc. The observation is due to Mates (1950). Scheffler (1955) discusses the matter more generally, and argues that no analysis of synonymy can suffice to explain the possibilities for substitution *salva veritate* in indirect discourse. There has been considerable discussion of these matters, but nothing, so far as I know, to affect the point at issue here.

expression appears in the context of (36) at the level
of structure at which these expressions (e.g., (33)-(35))
differ

In the semantically based theory, these three conditions lead to a
contradiction; by (37ii), the sentences S_{33}, S_{34}, S_{35} differ in semantic
representation (representation at the level of K-initial structures)
whereas (37i) and (37iii) imply that they must be represented
identically at this level, the differences of surface form being
determined by optional rules that map semantic representations
onto linguistic expressions. In the standard theory, the contradiction
does not arise. The analogues of (37) are simultaneously satisfied
by: (i) rules which assign the same semantic interpretation to (33)-
(35); (ii) rules which make reference to the deep structure of the
item appearing in the context of (36) in determining the meaning.
Condition (37iii) then poses no problem.

To reject (37i) or (37ii) is to abandon the semantically-based
theory (or to deny the facts), since K-initial structures will no longer
have the properties of semantic representations. Therefore it is
necessary to reject (37iii), and to assume that the representation
of (36) at the level of K-initial structures (semantic representations)
depends on not just the meaning but also the form of the expression
that appears ultimately in the context of (36). But to make this
move[19] is in effect to accept the standard theory in a confusing
form; differences in deep structure will determine differences of
semantic interpretation. In any case, then, the semantically-based
alternative collapses.

As far as I can see, an argument of this sort can be advanced
against any variety of semantically-based grammar (what is sometimes called "generative semantics") that has been discussed, or
even vaguely alluded to in the linguistic literature. One has to
put this tentatively, because many of the proposals are rather vague.
However, at least this much is clear. Any approach to semantically-
based grammar will have to take account of this problem.

Do considerations of this sort refute the standard theory as well?

[19] Assuming, that is, that it is possible to give it an intelligible formulation.

The example just cited is insufficient to refute the standard theory, since (33)-(35) differ in deep structure, and it is at least conceivable that "realize" and similar items can be defined so as to take account of this difference. Interesting questions arise when the matter is pursued further. Thus is it possible for someone to realize that John is believed to be incompetent by everyone without realizing that everyone believes John to be incompetent, or to realize that Bill saw John but not that John was seen by Bill? Or, suppose that John happens to speak a language just like English in relevant respects, except that it has no word translatable as *uncle*. What, then, is the status of S_{33} as compared to S_{34} and S_{35}? Or, consider such sentences as *everyone agrees that if John realizes that p, then he realizes that —*, where the space is filled either by *p* itself or by an expression *q* distinct from but synonymous with *p*. No doubt the truth value may change, as *q* replaces *p*, indicating that any difference of form of an embedded sentence can, in certain cases at least, play a role in the statement of truth conditions, hence, presumably, the determination of meaning. It remains to be determined whether there is some interesting subclass of such cases in which differences of deep structure suffice to account for the meaning differences, as the standard theory would require. If this could be shown, then the standard theory could still be maintained in a modified form: namely, except for cases in which ANY aspect of form may play a role in determining meaning. Instead of pursuing such questions as this, however, I would like to turn to another set of problems that seem to pose serious difficulties for the standard theory (and, a fortiori, for any variant of "generative semantics"). I have in mind cases in which semantic interpretation seems to relate more directly to surface structure than to deep structure.[20]

Consider such sentences as (38):

[20] The material in the remainder of this paper is drawn in large part from lectures given in Tokyo, in the summer of 1966, and prior to that, at MIT and UCLA. I am indebted to many of those who attended for comments and suggestions. Many of these and related topics are discussed by Kraak (1967), where rather similar conclusions are reached independently. I will not consider here some intricate but quite relevant considerations presented in Partee (1968).

(38)   (a) is it JOHN who writes poetry?

(b) it isn't JOHN who writes poetry

Under normal intonation[21] the capitalized word receives main stress and serves as the point of maximal inflection of the pitch contour. A natural response to (38) might be, for example, (39):

(39)   No, it is BILL who writes poetry

The sentence (39) is a possible answer to (38a) and corroboration of (38b). The semantic representation of (38) must indicate, in some manner, that *John* is the FOCUS of the sentence and that the sentence expresses the PRESUPPOSITION that someone writes poetry. In the natural response, (39), the presupposition of (38) is again expressed, and only the focus differs. On the other hand, a response such as (40) does not express the presupposition of (38):[22]

---

[21] The concept "normal intonation" is far from clear, but I will not try to explicate it here. I am assuming that the phonological component of the grammar contains rules that assign an intonation contour in terms of surface structure, along the lines discussed in Chomsky and Halle (1968). Special grammatical processes of a poorly-understood sort may apply in the generation of sentences, marking certain items (perhaps, even syllables of lexical items) as bearing specific expressive or contrastive features that will shift the intonation center, as in *is it John who writes POETRY* or *is it John who WRITES poetry*, etc. I am assuming that no such processes apply in (38). Sentences which undergo these processes are distinct in semantic interpretation, and perhaps in syntactic properties as well. Given the obscure nature of these matters, it is difficult to say anything more definite. The matter is further obscured by the fact that these processes, however they are to be described, may assign an extra-heavy stress and extra-dominant pitch to the item that would serve as intonation center under normal intonation—i.e., in the case where these processes do not apply. Quite possibly, these processes are to be described in general as superimposing a new contour on the normal one. Thus in *It ISN'T John who writes poetry* the word *John* retains its intonational prominence with respect to the following phrase, exactly as under normal intonation.

[22] A response such as (40) does not deny the presuppositon of (38), but rather its relevance. Again, these matters are far from clear, and deserve much fuller study than they have so far received. There is no reason to suppose that a satisfactory characterization of focus and presupposition can be given in purely grammatical terms, but there is little doubt that grammatical structure plays a part in specifying them. For some discussion of these matters in the case of cleft sentences such as (38), see Akmajian (1968).

(40)   No, John writes only short STORIES

In the case of (38), the underlying deep structure might be something like (41):[23]

(41)   [the one who writes poetry] is John

If so, then it would be natural to try to determine the focus and presupposition directly from the deep structure, in accordance with the standard theory, the focus being the predicate of the dominant proposition of the deep structure. Alternatively, one might propose that the focus is determined by the surface structure, namely, as the phrase containing the intonation center.
    Consider next (42):

(42)   (a) does John write poetry in his STUDY?
        (b) is it in his STUDY that John writes poetry?
        (c) John doesn't write poetry in his STUDY
        (d) it isn't in his STUDY that John writes poetry

Again, a natural response might be (43):

(43)   No, John writes poetry in the GARDEN

The sentences of (42) have as focus *study* (or *in his study*) and express the presupposition that John writes poetry somewhere, a presupposition also expressed in the normal response (43). To accommodate these facts within the standard theory, we might take (42b) and (42d) to have a deep structure rather like (41), with the predicate of the dominant sentence being *in his study*, say (44):

(44)   the place where John writes poetry is in his study

Again, the predicate expresses the focus and the embedded sentence the presupposition. To extend this analysis to (42a) and (42c), we would have to argue that the underlying structure of *John writes poetry in his study* is also something like (44), contrary to what is

[23] Following Akmajian, *ibid.* Alternatively, one might argue that the deep structure is of the form: [*it-one writes poetry*] *is John*, with the rule of extra-position giving *it is John who writes poetry*. The difference is immaterial, in the context of this discussion.

assumed in Chomsky (1965) and many earlier realizations of the standard theory, in which the phrase *in the study* is taken to be an adverbial modifier in a deep structure containing only one clause.[24]

In the case of (42), once again, an apparent alternative would be to determine focus and presupposition in terms of surface structure: the focus is the phrase containing the intonation center, and the presupposition is determined by replacement of the focus by a variable (we overlook, for the moment, a fundamental equivocation in the latter formulation).

To assist in the choice between these alternatives, it is useful to consider some more complex sentences. Thus consider (45):

(45)

$$\left\{ \begin{array}{l} \text{was it} \\ \text{it wasn't} \end{array} \right\} \left\{ \begin{array}{ll} \text{an ex-convict with a red SHIRT} & \text{(a)} \\ \text{a red-shirted EX-CONVICT} & \text{(b)} \\ \text{an ex-convict with a shirt that is red} & \text{(c)} \end{array} \right\} \text{that he}$$

was warned to look out for

The immediately underlying structure might be (46):

---

[24] This and related proposals are developed, on essentially these grounds, in Lakoff (1965). In more recent publications, other evidence has been cited to support an analysis along the lines of (44) for sentences like (42a), (42c). Thus Lakoff (1967) points out that we can say such things as *Goldwater won in Arizona, but it couldn't have happened in New York*, where *it* refers to Goldwater's winning, suggesting that *Goldwater won* is a sentential element in deep structure. However, the force of this argument is weakened by the fact that it would, if followed consistently, also lead us to the conclusion that in simple NVN sentences, the subject and verb constitute a sentence in deep structure (cf. *John turned the hot dog down flat, but it (that) wouldn't have happened with filet mignon; half the class flunked physics, which would never have happened in English Literature*). Not only is this an unsatisfactory consequence in itself, but it also leads to an apparent contradiction since the same argument yields the conclusion that the verb and object constitute a sentence (cf. *John turned the hot dog down flat, but it wouldn't have happened with Bill (as recipient); half the freshman class flunked physics, which would never have happened with the senior class*). Similarly, we would have to conclude that in the sentence *10 ERRORS WERE COMMITTED by the Red Sox and the Yankees in the game yesterday, but it (that) would never happen with any 2 other teams*, the capitalized expression constitutes a sentence in deep structure. I am aware of no strong argument for the analysis of (42a), (42c) with a deep structure like (44), except for the argument involving presuppositions.

(46)   the one he was warned to look out for was X,

where X is one of the phrases in the second pair of braces in (45). In this case, both the predicate phrase of (46) and the embedded clause of the subject must be further analyzed to reach the deep structure.

If it is deep structure that determines focus and presupposition along the lines indicated above, then the focus of the sentences of (45) should be (47), which are close or exact paraphrases of one another, and the presupposition should be (48):

(47)   (i) an ex-convict with a red shirt
        (ii) a red-shirted ex-convict
        (iii) an ex-convict with a shirt that is red
(48)   he was warned to look out for someone

Correspondingly, a natural response to any of (45) would be (49):

(49)   No, he was warned to look out for an AUTOMOBILE salesman

This conclusion is quite satisfactory, but there are difficulties when we explore further. Thus consider (50a-c):

(50)   (a) No, he was warned to look out for an ex-convict with a red TIE
        (b) No, he was warned to look out for a red-shirted AUTOMOBILE salesman
        (c) No, he was warned to look out for an ex-convict with a shirt that is GREEN

(50a), (50b), and (50c) are natural responses to (45a), (45b) and (45c), respectively; however, these are the only natural pairings. Thus (50a) could be a response to (45b) only in the sense in which (40) is a response to (38), that is by a denial of the relevance of the presupposition of (45b). In the case of (42), it was possible to maintain the standard theory by a modification of proposed deep structures. In the case of (45), however, this is quite impossible, without great artificiality. On the other hand, the facts just noted are accounted for directly by the alternative conception of focus and presupposition as determined by the intonation center of surface structure. According to this conception, the focus of (45a) can be taken as any of the phrases (51), and the corresponding presupposition is expressed by replacement of the focus by a variable:

(51)   (i) an ex-convict with a red shirt
       (ii) with a red shirt
       (iii) a red shirt
       (iv) shirt

all of the phrases of (51) contain the intonation center in (45a); hence each, in this conception, can be taken as focus. Correspondingly, any of (52) can be a natural response:

(52)   (i) No, he was warned to look out for an AUTOMOBILE salesman
       (ii) No, he was warned to look out for an ex-convict wearing DUNGAREES
       (iii) No, he was warned to look out for an ex-convict with a CARNATION
       (iv) No, he was warned to look out for an ex-convict with a red TIE

But (50b) and (50c) are not natural responses preserving presupposition in this sense. Similar comments apply to (45b) and (45c).

To shed further light on the matter, consider the sentences (53), which are related to (45a) as (42a, c) are related to (42b, d):

(53) $\begin{Bmatrix} \text{was he} \\ \text{he wasn't} \end{Bmatrix}$ (warned to (look out for (an ex-convict with (a red (SHIRT))))))

The phrases enclosed in paired parentheses are the phrases containing the intonation center (certain questions of detail aside). Each of these phrases can be taken as the focus of the sentence, so that natural responses would include, in addition to (52), the following:

(54)   (i) No, he was warned to expect a visit from the FBI

(ii) No, he was simply told to be more cautious

(iii) No, nothing was said to anyone[25]

In each case, the presupposition can be determined by replacing what is taken as focus by an appropriate variable. There may be no actual sentence expressing just this presupposition, for grammatical reasons, just as there is no cleft sentence corresponding to the choice of focus, in many cases (hence the qualification of p. 91. For example, (45a) can be interpreted with *shirt* as focus (so that (50a) is a natural response), but there is no grammatical sentences *it was* SHIRT *that he was warned to look out for an exconvict with a red*. Similarly, there is no grammatical sentence expressing exactly the presupposition of (45a) with the phrase *with a red shirt*, taken as focus.

Observe, in fact, that the focussed phrase need not correspond to a phrase of deep structure at all. This is clear in the case of (53), or, in a simpler case, (55):

(55) $\begin{Bmatrix} \text{is John} \\ \text{John isn't} \end{Bmatrix}$ (certain (to WIN)))

Natural responses would be any of (56):

(56)   (a) No, John is certain to LOSE

(b) No, John is likely not even to be NOMINATED

(c) No, the election will never take PLACE

[25] For naturalness, question and answer (or denial and corroboration) must not only share presuppositions, but also must use as focus items that are somehow related—exactly how is not clear, but the relation surely involves considerations that extend beyond grammar. Similar considerations arise in the case of natural coordination. For this reason, a pairing of sentences that might be expected on the formal grounds we are discussing may still not be natural, in the intuitive sense we are attempting to explicate. In other words, as in the case of coordination, grammatical (including semantic) considerations can suffice only for partial explication of certain intuitions that clearly involve other cognitive structures as well. Thus—to take a concrete example—if we were to rank sentences in order of naturalness as responses to (55), we would rank (56a) higher than $(\alpha) = No, he is certain to drink BEER$ or $(\beta) = No, he is EXPECTED to win$. However, if the present argument is correct, the nonnaturalness of (α) as a response to (55) is a matter of pairing of foci, whereas the nonnaturalness of (β) is a matter of determination of focus by intonation center.

Hence any of the parenthesized phrases of (55) can be taken as focus, but one, *certain to win*, corresponds to no element of deep structure if, as seems correct, the deep structure is something like (57) (with, perhaps, a specification of negation or question):

(57)   [s John win]s is certain

Similarly, consider the slightly more complex case (58):

(58) $\begin{cases} \text{is John} \\ \text{John isn't} \end{cases}$ believed to be certain to WIN

Evidently, *certain to win* is again a proper choice of focus, in which case what is presupposed is that something is believed of John. If we were to try to construct a cleft sentence corresponding to this interpretation of (58), it would have to be (59), analogous to (60):

(59)   it is certain to WIN that John is believed to be

(60)   it is $\begin{cases} \text{a homicidal MANIAC} \\ \text{INCOMPETENT} \end{cases}$ that John is believed to be

In all such cases, the cleft sentence is very marginal, or even totally unacceptable, from a strictly grammatical point of view, though it is certainly interpretable, presumably by analogy to properly formed sentences. In these deviant sentences as well there is an alternative natural choice of focus, namely, *to win* (in (58)) and *maniac* (in (60)).

Continuing to restrict ourselves to normal intonation — that is, the intonation defined by processes such as those described in Chomsky and Halle (1968) — consider the following sentences:

(61)   did the Red Sox play the YANKEES
(62)   (i) did the Red Sox beat the YANKEES
         (ii) were the Yankees beaten by the RED SOX

Sentence (61) can be interpreted as a question about whom the Red Sox played, about what they did, or about what happened. Thus possible answers might be any of (63):

(63)   (i) No, the TIGERS

(ii) No, they flew to WASHINGTON
(iii) No, the game never took PLACE

Thus (61) can be interpreted as presupposing that the Red Sox played someone (but whom?), that they did something (but what?), or that something happened (but what?) — the most natural interpretation perhaps being the first. The phrases containing the intonation center in the surface structure determine focus and presupposition. In the case of (62), there is no reason to suppose that there is any relevant difference in deep structure between (i) and (ii). The expressions of (63) are possible answers to (62i) and (62ii) but are, of course, differently interpreted in cases (63i) and (63ii).[26] It would, for example, be impossible to answer (62ii) by saying: *No, the Red Sox beat the TIGERS.* Or, to be more precise, this would be an answer only in the sense in which (40) is an answer to (38), that is, by failure to accept the presupposition.

Consider next the sentences (64):

(64)   (i) did John give the book to BILL
        (ii) did John give Bill the BOOK

The response *No, he kept it* is natural in both cases, since in each the phrase *give ...* is a possible focus; but (65i) is a presupposition-sharing response only for (64i), and (65ii) only for (64ii):

(65)   (i) No, to someone ELSE
        (ii) No, something ELSE

Thus although there is no relevant difference in deep structure between (64i) and (64ii), they differ in the range of possible focus and presupposition in the way predicted by the position of intonation center. The same observations hold of pairs such as *John didn't argue with Bill about MONEY, John didn't argue about money with BILL*, or *I didn't buy that car in Italy five YEARS ago, I didn't buy that car five years ago in ITALY*, etc. Similarly, in the case of such

[26]   In this case, (63ii) seems to me the least natural, presumably, because of the pairing of the concepts *win - lose* in the case of (62i), and because of the pairing of the action *flying to Washington* with the nonaction *being beaten by the Red Sox*, in the case of (62ii). See note 25.

a sentence as *I didn't buy that car five years ago in a country shaped like a BOOT*, there are additional natural responses, conforming to the same principle. The same is true if we consider such sentences as (66):

(66) (i) the question is not whether I should argue about money with BILL
      (ii) the question is not whether I should argue with Bill about MONEY

In the case of either, a natural response is: *it is whether I should go to England*. But when the focus is taken more narrowly, the sentences are seen to differ in the range of permissible focus and presupposition.

Further support for this general point of view comes from sentences in which, for reasons having to do with particular formatives, the intonation contour shifts. Thus consider (67) and (68):

(67) I didn't CATCH him
(68) (i) hard work doesn't mature TEEN-agers
      (ii) hard work doesn't MATURE people

In the case of (67), the focus can be *catch* or *catch him*, as distinct from *I didn't catch BILL*, where it can be *Bill* or *catch Bill*. In the case of (68i), the focus can be *teen-agers* or *mature teenagers* *(No, it matures only adults, No, it only makes anyone tired)*, whereas in the case of (68ii) it can be *mature* or *mature people* *(No, it harms them, No, it only makes anyone tired)*. In fact, even in the simplest sentences similar observations hold. Thus *Brutus killed CAESAR* can be used to state what Brutus did or who Brutus killed, whereas *Brutus KILLED him* can be used to state what Brutus did or what Brutus did to him. And so on, in many other cases.

So far I have restricted attention to cases of "normal intonation", this being understood tentatively as referring to cases in which the intonation contour is determined by rules of the sort discussed in Chomsky and Halle (1968), with no expressive or contrastive intonation marked in specific expressions by other grammatical processes (see note 21). Turning our attention briefly to cases of the latter sort, it appears that similar conclusions follow. Consider, for example, (69), which differs from (66) in that the intonation center is shifted to the negative element.

(69)   (i) the question is NOT whether I should argue about money with Bill
        (ii) the question is NOT whether I should argue with Bill about money

Assuming that the intonation is otherwise normal, it still seems to be true, as in the case of (66), that (70i) is a natural response to (69i) but not (69ii), and that (70ii) is a natural response to (69ii) but not (69i):

(70)   (i) No, (it is whether I should argue about money) with MARY
        (ii) No, (it is whether I should argue with Bill) about his trip to EUROPE

On the other hand, *No, it is whether I should go to England* is a natural response to either (i) or (ii) of (69). In all these cases, the assertion (69) is corroborated. This observation (and the analogous observation in the other instances discussed above) supports the suggestion in note 21 that in some cases, at least, expressive or contrastive stress superimposes a new contour, preserving the arrangement of focus and presupposition defined by the normal intonation. The factual judgments appear to me quite insecure, however.

Consider next such cases as (71):

(71)   did John give the BOOK to Bill

In this case, as distinct from the case of normal intonation (64i), the natural response is (65ii), not (65i). On the other hand, the sentence *No, he kept it* seems much less natural as a response to (71) than to either case of (64). This observation (and its analogue in other cases) suggests that when expressive or contrastive stress shifts intonation center, the same principle applies as in normal cases for determining focus and presupposition, but with the additional proviso that naturalness declines far more sharply as larger and larger phrases containing the intonation center are considered as a possible focus. This would be a very natural interpretation of contrastive or expressive intonation, and it seems consistent with a number of relatively clear cases, at least. Hence it may perhaps be proposed as a first approximation to a general interpretive theory for this phenomenon. The same seems to me to be true when extra-emphasis is given to the item that contains the normal intonation center. Again, the factors mentioned in note 25 seem relevant.

The processes involved in determining contrastive or expressive intonation at the moment do not appear to be germane to this discussion. However, it is worth noting that they cannot be described, at least in any natural way, in terms of deep structure. This becomes most obvious when we consider positions in which there MUST be a contrastive intonation. Thus consider the sentence (72):

(72)   John is neither EASY to please, nor EAGER to please, nor CERTAIN to please, nor INCLINED to please, nor HAPPY to please, ...

In "parallel constructions," in some sense of this notion that has never been made quite clear, contrastive intonation is necessary. But it is evident, in such examples as (72) at least, that it is a parallelism of surface structure, not deep structure, that is involved. The point is even clearer when we consider such sentences as (73):

(73)   John is more concerned with AFfirmation than with CONfirmation

Here, the parallelism requires even a shift in contour within a single word. There are many similar cases.

To summarize these remarks, we seem to have the following situation. Rules of phonological interpretation assign an intonational contour to surface structures. Certain phrases of the surface structure may be marked, by grammatical processes of a poorly-understood sort, as receiving expressive or contrastive stress, and these markings also affect the operation of the rules of phonological interpretation. If no such processes have applied, the rules assign the normal intonation. In any event, phrases that contain the intonation center may be interpreted as focus of utterance, the condition perhaps being somewhat different and more restrictive when the intonation center involves expressive or contrastive stress, as noted. Choice of focus determines the relation of the utterance to responses, to utterances to which it is a possible response, and to other sentences in the discourse. The notions "focus", "presupposition", and "shared presupposition" (even in cases where the presupposition may not be expressible by a grammatical sentence)[27] must be determinable from the semantic interpretation of sentences if we are to be able to explain how discourse is constructed and, in general, how language is used.

In many cases, it seems that we can interpret a sentence in these terms, given the intonation center, in the following way. The focus is a phrase containing the intonation center; the presupposition, an expression derived by replacing the focus by a variable. Each sentence, then, is associated with a class of pairs (F, P) where F is a focus and P a presupposition, each such pair corresponding to one possible interpretation. In terms of these notions we can begin to explicate such notions as natural (presupposition-sharing) response. Thus for a sentence S interpreted as (F, P) to be a natural response to a sentence S' interpreted as (F', P'), it must be the case that P = P'. Furthermore, F and F' must be paired in some "natural" way, where the relevant concept of "naturalness" no doubt extends beyond grammar, in the broadest sense of the con-

---

[27] Note that we are using the term "presupposition" to cover a number of notions that should be distinguished. Thus *it was JOHN who was here* expresses the presupposition that someone was here in the sense that truth of the presupposition is a prerequisite for the utterance to have a truth value. On the other hand, when we replace one of the foci of *John gave Bill the BOOK* by a variable, it is not at all clear that the resulting expression determines a presupposition in the same sense, though it does characterize "what the utterance asserts" and to which utterances it is a proper response, when so understood.

cept "grammar". Further elaborations of these notions are surely in order,[28] but this seems in general a fair first approximation. In the present context, I wish only to emphasize that these notions seem to involve surface structure in an essential way, and thus to provide strong counter-evidence to the standard theory, which stipulates that semantic interpretation must be entirely determined by deep structure.

There is one obvious way to preserve the standard theory in the face of considerations of the sort just discussed, namely, to set the rule (74) as the first rule of the grammar, where F and P are arbitrary structures and S′ functions as the initial symbol of the categorial component of the base:

(74) $S \rightarrow S'$ F P

Continuing to generate a full syntactic and phonological structure in accordance with the standard theory, we would then add a new "filtering rule", namely, that the structure generated is well-formed only if the focus and presupposition, as determined from surface structure, are identical with F and P, respectively. Technically, it would now be the case that deep structure fully determines meaning,

---

[28]   For example, the focus must be composed of full lexical items — more generally, items that make a contribution to the meaning of a sentence that is in some sense independent of anything outside the focus. In particular, the syllable containing the intonation center cannot serve as focus when it is part of a larger lexical item (except under the rather different circumstances of contrastive stress, as illustrated by (73)). Similarly, in a sentence such as *Did you call him UP*, the item *up* cannot serve as focus, but only *call him up* or the full proposition; and in *Did you take it for GRANTED*, neither *granted* nor *for granted*, but only *take it for granted* (or the full proposition) can be taken as focus. This is an obvious condition to be placed on the motion of "focus", given the role it plays in explaining how sentences are used and interpreted. The same can be said of idioms in general. Hence determination of focus must involve reference to the lexicon (and, no doubt, an associated idiom list). This seems to pose no special problem. There are, incidentally, many questions that can be raised about exactly how an idiom list should be related to a grammar, but these, so far as I can see, have no bearing on the topic under discussion; nor is there, for the moment, any interesting published suggestion about this matter, to my knowledge, though an approach suggested by Fraser (1968) shows promise. I am grateful to M. Bierwisch for bringing these facts to my attention.

even so far as focus and presupposition is concerned.[29] Thus underlying (75i) we would have structures with the phrase-marker for *the book, give John the book,* and *Bill gives John the book* as focus and corresponding presuppositions; and underlying (75ii) we would have structures with the phrase-marker for *John, give the book to John* and *Bill gives the book to John* as focus with corresponding presuppositions; but not conversely, given the well-formedness condition.

(75)   (i) did Bill give John the BOOK
         (ii) did Bill give the book to JOHN

Obviously, this is merely a notational variant of a theory that determines focus and presupposition from the surface structure. In fact, the F and P positions would have to accommodate structures that can only be derived by transformation (as, e.g., in cases such as (55) and (72) and others where the focus is transformationally derived). The rules (74) and the associated filtering condition are redundant, since they are determined, by a general interpretive principle, from the structure generated in the usual way when these extra formal concepts are eliminated. If we were willing to permit such formal devices, then the claim of the standard theory that deep structure fully determines semantic interpretation would be vacuous; if we do not permit them, it seems to be false.

Observe that these considerations do not touch on one aspect of the standard theory, namely, the hypothesis that the grammatical relations that enter into semantic interpretation are those represented in deep structure. In fact, it seems to me that insofar as the standard theory is plausible in its approach to semantic interpretation, it is with respect to this specific hypothesis. Thus it is natural to suppose that the meaning of a sentence is determined by minimal meaning-bearing elements and the relations into which they enter, these relations being specified in part by the lexicon

---

[29] It is worth noting that the proposal discussed earlier to determine the focus as the predicate of the dominant sentence of the deep structure is not very different from this proposal.

itself and in part by the rules of the categorial component. But this narrower hypothesis remains unchallenged by the consideration of focus and presupposition. On the other hand, the attempt to express the latter concepts in terms of deep structure seems to me to have led to considerable artificiality in the construction of grammars, in recent work.

Turning to related questions, it was suggested a number of years ago by Kuroda (1965) that the position of such elements as *even* and *only* is determined by transformational processes, rather than by rules of the base, and that their contribution to the meaning of the sentences in which they appear is determined by their position in surface structure. That their position is determined by transformational processes is suggested by the fact that there are "global" constraints on their occurrence; for example, *only* or *even* can appear in any of the blanks of (76), but it is questionable whether they can appear in more than one of these positions.

(76)   — John — reads — books on politics

In particular, neither *only* or *even* can occur in all of these positions. But constraints of this sort are transformational rather than "phrase-structural" in character. Furthermore, the meaning of the sentence evidently changes as *even* or *only* takes one or the other position. Kuroda suggests, then, that there is a certain category of transformations — which he calls "attachment transformations" — that do affect meaning, in the way indicated.[30]

More recently, Jackendoff has argued in a number of important papers that many semantic phenomena can be explained most readily in terms of features of surface structure. In particular, he suggests (1968) that the scope of logical elements such as negation and quantifiers is determined by surface structure. Thus consider such sentences as (77):

(77)   (i) not many arrows hit the target
        (ii) many arrows didn't hit the target

---

[30] His primary examples have to do with the problem of the *wa-ga* distinction in Japanese. Examples such as (76) are somewhat questionable, as Susan Fischer has pointed out, because they also involve critically the placement of contrastive stress. See Fischer (1968), where a different analysis is proposed.

(iii) not many arrows didn't hit the target

It might perhaps be argued that (77iii) is ungrammatical, though (as in the case of many deviant sentences) one can, if required, impose a definite interpretation on it. If so, then placement of negation meets the "global conditions" that signify that a transformational process is involved. But, evidently, (77i) and (77ii) are quite different in meaning. Hence if we suppose that the underlying structure is (78) and that (77i) and (77ii) are derived by a *not*-placement rule (and (77iii) not directly generated at all), then the deep structure will not determine the meaning.

(78)   not [many arrows hit the target]

Rather, the scope of negation will be determined by the position of *not* in surface structure. In (77i), it is the proposition that many arrows hit the target that is denied. In (77ii), many arrows are asserted to have failed to hit the target; i.e., it is the verb phrase that is "negated". (Observe that whatever the status of (77iii) may be, the examples (77i, ii) suggest that scope of negation is determined by surface structure unless we were to permit *not* to appear in deep structure in association with the phrase that constitutes its "scope" — a conclusion that violates the standard theory when applied to the examples to which we turn next.)

In support of this analysis, Jackendoff notes the relation of meaning between active and passive forms involving both quantifiers and negation. Thus he considers the following sentences:

(79)   the target was not hit by many arrows
(80)   not many demonstrators were arrested by the police
(81)   many demonstrators were not arrested by the police
(82)   John didn't buy many arrows
(83)   many arrows were not bought by John
(84)   John bought not many arrows
(85)   not many arrows were bought by John

Sentence (79) is a paraphrase of (77i), not (77ii), to which it would be related by the simplest form of the passive operation. Correspondingly, the order of quantifier and negation is the same in the surface structure of the paraphrases (77i) and (79), but different in (77ii). Furthermore, (77ii) has no passive paraphrase. What is suggested by (77)-(79), then, is that the order of quantifier and negation in the surface structure determines the meaning. Consequently, if the surface subject has a quantifier, then sentence negation (such as (77i)) will be different in meaning from verb phrase negation (such as (77ii)); but if the quantifier is part of a noun phrase that follows the verb, then the order of negation and quantifier is identical in sentence negation and verb phrase negation, and the meanings will be the same.

This principle is supported by (80), (81). The subject contains a quantifier, and correspondingly the case (80) of sentence negation differs in meaning from the case (81) of verb phrase negation, since the order of quantifier and negation is different. This principle is further supported by examples (82)-(85). Sentences (82) and (83) are obviously different in meaning, though (84) and (85) are the same in meaning[31] as are (82) and (85). In (82), (84), (85) the order of negation and quantifier is the same; in (83), the order differs. This is as required by the principle just stated.

According to this principle, sentence negation will differ in meaning from verb phrase negation in case the surface subject contains a quantifier, that is, in case the order of negation and quantifier differs in the two cases. Since it is the notion "surface subject" that is involved in determining sameness or difference of meaning, the principle is inconsistent with the standard theory. Furthermore, the principle of interpretation of surface structures seems clear, and, in addition, the transformations that form passives can be left in a simple form (though they will drastically

---

[31] Assuming, that is, that (84) is well-formed. The question is actually irrelevant, having to do with the transformational source of (85) rather than the principle in question. It is sufficient to point out that (82) (under the most natural interpretation) is a paraphrase of (85). Under a less natural, but perhaps possible interpretation, it might be taken as *there are many arrows that John didn't buy*, a possibility that is irrelevant here because it remains consistent with the assumption that surface structure determines scope of negation, though it does not provide evidence for this assumption as do the other examples discussed.

change meaning, if they change the order of quantifier and negation). These facts, then, provide strong support for the hypothesis
that surface structure determines (in part, at least) the scope of
logical elements, and serve as strong counter-evidence to the
standard theory in its most general form. Conceivably, one might
modify the standard theory to accommodate these facts, but this
modification would be justified (assuming it possible) just in case
it achieved the naturalness and explanatory force of Jackendoff's
proposal that negation and quantifiers are associated with phrases
of the surface structure, and their interpretation is determined by
the phrases in which they appear and their relative order. Jackendoff
shows that a number of other cases can be explained in the same
way.

Jackendoff's arguments, like those involving focus and presupposition, leave unaffected the hypothesis that the grammatical
relations defined in the deep structure are those that determine
semantic interpretation. If we modify the standard theory,
restricting in this way the contribution of the base to semantic
interpretation, we can take account of the fact that many aspects
of surface structure appear to play a role in determining semantic
interpretation; correspondingly, insofar as some development in
syntactic theory is motivated by the demand that these aspects of
semantic interpretation be expressed in deep structure, it will have
lost its justification. To mention one example, consider the
sentences (86):

(86)   (i) the sonata is easy to play on this violin
        (ii) this violin is easy to play the sonata on

These sentences share a single system of grammatical relations
and, in some reasonable sense of paraphrase, may be regarded as
paraphrases; they have the same truth conditions, for example.
However, they seem different in meaning in that one makes an
assertion about the sonata, and the other about the violin. Before
this difference is used to motivate a difference in deep structure,
however, it must be shown that this aspect of meaning is one

expressed in deep rather than surface structure. In the present instance, this conclusion seems at best dubious.[32]

Certain properties of modal auxiliaries also suggest a role for surface structure semantic interpretive rules. Thus J. Emonds has pointed out that *shall* is interpreted differently in question and corresponding declarative.

(87)　(i) I shall go downtown
　　　(ii) shall I go downtown
　　　(iii) I $\begin{Bmatrix} \text{asked} \\ \text{wonder} \end{Bmatrix}$ whether I shall go downtown

In (87i) and (87iii), the modal is essentially a tense marker. In (87ii), however, it has a very different meaning, namely, the meaning of *should*. In general, interrogative expressions such as (87ii) have the same meaning as the corresponding embedded expression in sentences of the form (87iii), and, in fact, this observation, appropriately extended, has been used to support the syntactic derivation of interrogatives from embedded interrogative clauses (see, e.g., Katz and Postal, 1964). However, in the case of (87), this expectation is not verified. If we assume that the sentences of (87) are related as are those derived by replacing *shall* by *will*, or by perfect aspect, etc., then the standard theory in its strongest form is refuted. If, furthermore, we wish to maintain the weaker hypothesis that the semantically functioning grammatical relations are those represented in deep structure, then we must conclude that the relation of *I* to *shall* in (87) is not a grammatical relation in this sense — it is not, for example, the subject-predicate relation. This seems a natural enough conclusion.

Other examples involving modals immediately come to mind. Thus it has frequently been noted that (88i) and (88iii) merely

---

[32] What is involved, apparently, is a relation of topic-comment which must be distinguished from that of subject-predicate. See Chomsky (1965), for some brief discussion within the framework of the standard theory of a question with a long history. Other arguments for distinguishing (86i) and (86ii) at the deep structure level have been proposed in recent work (e.g., Perlmutter, 1968), but they seem to me unpersuasive, though the interesting phenomena noted by Perlmutter must certainly be accounted for.

predict, whereas (88ii) is ambiguous, in that it may also mean that
John refuses to go downtown:

(88)   (i) John will go downtown
        (ii) John won't go downtown
        (iii) it is not the case that John will go downtown

Again, the interplay of negation and modal seems a natural
candidate for a principle of surface structure interpretation.[33] Or
consider such sentences as (89) (also pointed out by Emonds):

(89)   John can't seem to get his homework done on time

There is no corresponding form without *not*. Furthermore, the
modal is interpreted as associated with an underlying embedded
proposition *John gets his homework done on time*. Hence if *can*
appears in deep structure in association with *seem*, as it appears in
association with *work* in *John can't work*, then a rule of surface
structure interpretation is needed to account for its semantic
relation to the embedded verbal phrase *get* .... Suppose, on the
other hand, that *can* appears at the deep structure level in association with the embedded sentence *John gets his homework done on
time*.[34] Then a rule is necessary that extracts *can* from the embedded
sentence and assigns it to the matrix sentence — in fact, to exactly
the position it occupies in simple sentences. However, note that
this extraction is possible only when *can* is interpreted as indicating
ability, not possibility. Thus (89) has approximately the sense of
(90), but the sentence (91), if grammatical at all, surely does not
have the sense of (92):

---

[33] Examples such as (88ii) have been used to justify the argument that there
are two sources for *will* (and other modals as well). The arguments in general
seem to me unconvincing, since an alternative formulation involving rules of
interpretation is immediately available. Furthermore, it seems that the phenomena observed are of some generality. Thus the difference in meaning between (88ii) and (88i,iii) is characteristic of the future "tense" in many languages,
and thus has nothing to do, apparently, with the volitional force of the
element *will*.

[34] A conclusion which appears implausible in that in general *to*-VP constructions, as in (89), exclude modals.

(90)   it seems $\begin{cases} \text{that John can't get his homework done on time} \\ \text{that John is unable to get his homework done} \\ \text{on time} \end{cases}$

(91)   the war can't seem to be ended by these means

(92)   it seems $\begin{cases} \text{that the war can't be ended by these means} \\ \text{that it is impossible for the war to be ended by} \\ \text{these means} \end{cases}$

Hence either the extraction operation will have to be sensitive to the difference in sense of two cases of *can* — an otherwise unmotivated complication — or else the interpretation will have to be "delayed" until after extraction has taken place. The latter choice requires a rule of interpretation that does not apply to deep structure.

Notice that in general rules of semantic interpretation have a "filtering function" analogous to that of rules of transformation in the standard theory. This is true no matter at what level they apply. Thus a rule of interpretation applying at the deep structure level may assign an anomalous interpretation to an otherwise well-formed sentence. A rule of interpretation that applies to other structures of the class K of syntactic structures, say to surface structures, may have the same effect, in principle. Thus a decision that *can* in (89) appears at the deep structure level in association with *seem* would not be refuted by the observation that (91) is deviant; rather, the deviance, in this view, would be attributed to the filtering function of a principle of semantic interpretation applying at the surface structure level.

Anaphoric processes constitute another domain where it is reasonable to inquire into the possibility that rules of semantic interpretation operate at the level of surface structure. It has been noted by Akmajian and Jackendoff (1968) that stress plays a role in determining how the reference of pronouns is to be interpreted. For example, in the sentence (93), *him* refers to Bill if it is unstressed, but it may refer either to John or to someone other than John or Bill if it is stressed:

(93)   John hit Bill and then George hit him

Similarly, in (94), where *else* is stressed, *someone else* refers to someone other than John, whereas when *afraid* is stressed, it refers to John himself:

(94)   John washed the car; I was afraid someone else would do it

The same phenomenon can be observed within sentence boundaries. The explanation hinges on the analysis of placement of primary stress, but it is reasonable to suppose, as Akmajian and Jackendoff suggest, that a principle of surface structure interpretation is involved, given what is known about the relation of intonation to surface structure. See also Jackendoff (1967).

Recent observations by Ray Dougherty (1968a, b) lend some support to this proposal. He argues that the interpretive rules of reference must apply after the application of various transformations, making use of information that is not present at the deep structure level. Thus consider the sentences (95):

(95)   (i) each of the men hates his brothers
           (ii) the men each hate his brothers

Dougherty gives considerable evidence to support the view that (95ii) is derived from a structure such as (95i), by a rule that moves *each* to one of several possible positions in a sentence. But clearly (i) and (ii) differ in the range of possible interpretations for the reference of the pronoun *he*. Thus in (ii), but not (i), it is necessary to interpret *he* as referring to someone other than the men in question. The deviance of (96ii), then, might be attributed to the filtering effect of rules of surface structure interpretation:

(96)   (i) each of the men hates his own brothers
           (ii) the men each hate his own brothers

Or, consider the sentences (97):

(97)   (i) each of Mary's sons hates his brothers
           (ii) his brothers are hated by each of Mary's sons
           (iii) his brothers hate each of Mary's sons
           (iv) each of Mary's sons is hated by his brothers

The simplest formulation of the passive transformation would derive (ii) from a structure like (i), and (iv) from a structure like (iii). But in (ii) and (iii), *he* cannot be interpreted as referring to any of Mary's sons, though in (i) and (iv) it can be so interpreted. As Dougherty points out in detail, there are many similar phenomena. The matter is not restricted to pronominalization; thus consider the effect of replacing *his* by *the other* in (97). There appears to be, in such cases, a relatively simple rule of interpretation which makes use of surface structure information, and which, with its filtering effect, rules that certain otherwise well-formed sentences are deviant. Such observations as these, then, also lend support to a revision of the standard theory that incorporates such rules.

Turning to still more obscure cases in which semantic interpretation may involve surface properties, consider the curious behavior of perfect aspect in English with respect to the presuppositions it expresses. Quite generally, a sentence such as (98) is taken as presupposing that John is alive:

(98)   John has lived in Princeton.

Thus knowing that (99) is true, one would not say *Einstein has lived in Princeton;* rather *Einstein lived in Princeton:*

(99)   Einstein has died[35]

But now consider the following sentences:

(100)   Einstein has visited Princeton
(101)   Princeton has been visited by Einstein

[35] As can be seen from (99), it is not invariably true that use of the present perfect aspect as the full auxiliary presupposes that the subject is alive, although (99) would nevertheless only be appropriate under rather special circumstances, e.g., if Einstein's death had just occurred. Where a verb can be used in the historical present, use of the present perfect does not seem to carry the presupposition that the subject is alive. Thus I could not say *Aristotle has visited Crete* or *Aristotle visits Crete* (in historical present), but there is no presupposition that Aristotle is alive in *Aristotle has claimed, investigated, demonstrated,...* (or in *Aristotle demonstrates in the* Posterior Analytics *that...,* etc.).

The example (98) is discussed in Chomsky (1970), p. 50, but with no reference to the full range of complexities involved.

(102) Einstein (among others) has told me that ...
(103) I have been told by Einstein (among others) that ...
(104) Einstein has taught me physics
(105) I have been taught physics by Einstein

It seems to me that (100), (102), (104) presuppose the denial of (99), but that (101), (103), and (105) do not. If this is correct, then the semantic interpretation of perfect aspect would appear to depend on certain properties of surface structure.[36]

The problem is still more complex when we consider coordinate and other constructions. Thus consider the following cases:

(106) Hilary has climbed Everest
(107) Marco Polo has climbed Everest
(108) Marco Polo and Hilary have climbed Everest
(109) Marco Polo and many others have climbed Everest
(110) Everest has been climbed by Marco Polo (among others)
(111) many people have climbed Everest

Sentences (106) and (107) express the presupposition that Hilary and Marco Polo, respectively, are alive.[37] On the other hand, sentences (108)-(110) do not express the presupposition that Marco Polo is

---

[36] Unless it is maintained that the surface subject of the passive is also the deep subject. Although arguments for this view can be advanced (see, e.g., Hasegawa, 1968), it seems to me incorrect, a strong counter-argument being provided by idioms that undergo passivization, moving to the surface subject position noun phrases which cannot otherwise appear as subject — e.g., *advantage was taken of Bill*, *offense was taken at that remark*, *a great deal of headway was made*, etc.

Notice, incidentally, that assumptions about whether the entity referred to by a noun phrase is alive can be related in rather complex ways to the structure of an utterance and the lexical items it contains. Thus if I say that John is a friend of mine or that I get along with John, the presupposition is that he is alive; but if I say that John is a hero of mine or that I admire him, this is no longer presupposed; as of course, it is not presupposed, in any of these cases, if present tense is replaced by past tense.

[37] It is even clearer, perhaps, in *Marco Polo has succeeded in climbing Everest*. However, for some obscure reason, it seems to me that if Hilary had just announced that he had succeeded in climbing Everest, it would have been appropriate, without the presupposition that Marco Polo is alive, to have said: *But Marco Polo has done it too*.

alive; and (111) expresses no such presupposition with regard to the various climbers of Everest. Intuitions about this matter do not appear too firm, but if the judgments just expressed are accurate, then it seems that surface structure must play a role in determining the presupposition of the utterance in a rather complex manner.

Significant differences in interpretation of sentences as the auxiliary is changed are very easy to demonstrate. Thus sentence (112) presupposes that John is a Watusi, but if we replace *is* by *would be*, the presupposition is that he is not:

(112) John is tall for a Watusi

Furthermore, (112) presupposes that the Watusi are generally not tall, but if *even* is inserted after *tall*, the presupposition is that the Watusi are tall, and it is asserted that John, who is a Watusi, is even taller than expected. If *even* precedes *John* in (112), the assertion is that John, who is a Watusi, is short, as are the Watusi in general. Thus the change in position of *even* changes the content with regard to the height of John and the standard height of the Watusi.

This by no means exhausts the class of cases where it appears reasonable to postulate rules of interpretation that make use of information not represented in deep structure. These cases suggest that the standard theory is incorrect, and that it should be modified to permit these rules. These considerations may not affect the weaker hypothesis that the grammatical relations represented in deep structure are those that determine semantic interpretation. However, it seems that such matters as focus and presupposition, topic and comment, reference, scope of logical elements, and perhaps other phenomena, are determined in part at least by properties of structures of K other than deep structures, in particular, by properties of surface structure. In short, these phenomena suggest that the theory of grammar should be reconstructed along the lines intuitively indicated in (113), using the notation of the earlier discussion:

(113) base: $(P_1, ..., P_i)$ (P_1 the K-initial, P_i the post-lexical (deep) structure of the syntactic structure which is a member of K)

transformations: $(P_i,\ldots, P_n)$ $(P_n$ the surface structure; $(P_1,\ldots, P_n)\varepsilon K)$
phonology: $P_n\rightarrow$phonetic representation
semantics: $(P_i, P_n)\rightarrow$semantic representation (the grammatical relations involved being those of P_i, that is, those represented in P_1).

Notice, incidentally, that it is, strictly speaking, not P_n that is subject to semantic interpretation but rather the structure determined by phonological interpretation of P_n, with intonation center assigned. We have already noted, in discussing the matter of "opaque" contexts, that it is impossible to construct a "semantically-based" syntax along the lines that have been proposed in recent discussion. See pp. 85-88. The phenomena that we have now been considering lend further support to this conclusion (unnecessary support, in that the earlier observations suffice to establish the conclusion). It must be borne in mind, however, that the proposed revision of the standard theory does not imply that grammar is "syntactically-based" in the sense that in generating a sentence one must "first" form P_1 by the categorial component, "then" forming P_i by lexical insertion, "then" forming the remainder of the syntactic structure $\Sigma\varepsilon K$ by transformation, "then" interpreting Σ by semantic and phonological rules. In fact, this description, whatever its intuitive suggestiveness, has no strict meaning, since the revised theory assigns no "order" to operations, just as the standard theory assigns no order of application, as already noted. In fact, there is nothing to prevent one from describing the standard theory or the proposed revision as characterizing grammars that map phonetic representation onto triples (deep structure, surface structure, phonetic representation), or as mapping pairs (phonetic representation, deep structure) onto pairs (surface structure, semantic representation), etc. In fact, the revision, like the standard theory, characterizes grammars that define a certain relation among these concepts, where the relation has properties determined by the precise nature of base rules, transformations, rules of phonological interpretation, and rules of semantic interpretation.

It may be useful, at this point, to recall the attempts of the past few years to study the relation of syntax and semantics within the framework of transformational-generative grammar. Within this framework, the first attempt to show how the syntactic structure of a sentence contributes to determining its meaning was that of Katz and Fodor (1963), an approach that was modified and extended in Katz and Postal (1964). The basic assumption was that meaning is determined by properties of phrase-markers and transformation-markers (P-markers and T-markers). In Katz and Fodor (1963), two types of rule of interpretation ("projection rule") were considered. Type 1 projection rules operate on configurations of P-markers; type 2 projection rules are associated with transformations and their configurations. In Katz and Postal (1964), it was argued that T-markers play no role in the determination of meaning. First, it was argued that obligatory transformations can in principle have no semantic effects, since "the output of sentences which result from such rules is fully determined by the input P-markers" (p. 31). Then, a variety of syntactic arguments were given to show that optional transformations also do not change meaning. It was further argued that only the configurations of underlying (base) P-markers are semantically relevant. We are left, then, with the conclusion that the only rules relevant to determination of meaning are the rules of the categorial component. This line of argument was accepted in most work done at about that time within the framework of transformational-generative grammar—including, in particular, Chomsky (1965).

Since surface structure is fully determined by base rules and transformational rules, it seems natural to suppose that properties of surface structure, not being a matter of "choice", could not contribute to semantic interpretation. Underlying this assumption one might perhaps discern the remnants of the "Saussurian" view that a sentence is constructed by a series of successive choices, and that each of these may be related to semantic considerations of some sort. Of course, such talk is only metaphorical when we are concerned with competence rather than performance. It may, however, have occasionally been misleading, suggesting, erroneously, that since surface structure is fully determined by other "choices", properties of surface structure cannot contribute to semantic interpretation. When we drop the loose and metaphoric use of such notions as "choice", we see that there is no reason at all why properties of surface structure should not play a role in determining semantic interpretation, and the considerations brought forward earlier suggest that in fact they do play such a role.

To conclude this discussion, I would like to take note of one additional line of investigation that appears to complement the study of semantic properties of surface structure. In outlining the standard theory (p. 65-68 above) I pointed out that it contained a well-formedness condition on surface structures, and thus implied that transformations have what has been called a "filtering function" (cf. Chomsky, 1965). In Ross (1967) there is further investigation of "output conditions" that serve as well-formedness conditions for surface structures. The conditions that Ross investigates are of a "graded" rather than an "all or none" character, recalling some interesting observations of Bolinger (1961). In Perlmutter (1968) it is demonstrated that there are also "output conditions" of a sort more typical of grammatical processes of the familiar kind, and it is shown that these conditions serve to enrich considerably the filtering effect of transformations. Joseph Emonds, in very interesting work now in progress, has amassed considerable evidence suggesting that the set of conditions on structures close to surface structure have properties expressible by a set of context-free phrase structure rules. Thus to mention just one typical example, he considers the observation in Chomsky (1970) that the passive transformation in English consists of two separate rules: a rule of subject-postposing that converts the structure underlying *John accept the proposal* into *accept the proposal by John;* and a subsequent rule of object-preposing that converts the latter into *the proposal accept by John.* Where the proposition in question is a nominal expression, subject-postposing may apply alone, giving ultimately *the acceptance of the proposal by John;* or both operations may apply, giving *the proposal's acceptance by John.* But where the proposition in question is a full sentence, it is necessary for both operations to apply, so that we have the sentence *the proposal was accepted by John* but not *was accepted the proposal by John* or *accept the proposal by John*. He points out that this discrepancy can be accounted for by a condition which we can formulate (departing now from Emonds' interpretation) as requiring that the set of surface structures (or, to be more precise those structures that precede the application of "last-cycle rules" such as auxiliary inversion, etc.) satisfy the rules of a phrase structure grammar that permits noun phrases of the form N-PP-PP (e.g., *the offer of a book to John*) but no sentences of the form V-NP-PP (an obligatory rule of *of*-insertion applies in the context N—NP). Some of Perlmutter's data also seem susceptible to such an analysis. From many examples of this sort, it is reasonable to propose a further modification of the standard theory, perhaps along these lines: a set of context-free rules generates structures that become surface structures by application of last-cycle transformational rules, and a related set (perhaps a subset of these) serves as the categorial component of the base; transformations map base structures into well-formed structures close to surface structures meeting the requirements of a phrase structure grammar. Such an extension of the standard theory, if warranted, would be an interesting and suggestive supplement to the proposal that properties of surface structure play a distinctive role in semantic interpretation. It seems to me that these ideas suggest a line of investigation which, though still unclear in many respects, may prove quite promising.

REFERENCES

Akmajian, A.
  1968 "On the analysis of cleft sentences", M.I.T.
Akmajian, A. and R. Jackendoff
  1968 "Squib", M.I.T.
Austin, J. L.
  1956 "A plea for excuses", *Proceedings of the Aristotelian Society*, 1956-7, Reprinted in J.D. Urmson and G.J. Warnock (eds.), *John L. Austin's Philosophical Papers* (Oxford, 1961).

Bolinger, D. L.
   1961   *Generality, Gradience, and the All-or-none* (= *Janua Linguarum* series minor, No. 14) (Mouton and Co., The Hague).
Bresnan, J.
   1968   "A note on instrumental adverbs and the concept of deep structure", M.I.T.
Chafe, W. L.
   1967   "Language as symbolization", *Language* 43, pp. 57-91.
Chomsky, N.
   1965   *Aspects of the Theory of Syntax*, M.I.T. Press.
   1970   "Remarks on Nominalization", in R. Jacobs and P. Rosenbaum (eds.), *Readings in English Transformational Grammar* (Ginn and Co). This volume, pp. 11-61.
Chomsky, N. and M. Halle
   1968   *Sound Pattern of English* (Harper and Row).
Dougherty, R.
   1968a   "A Transformational Grammar of Coordinate Conjoined Structures", Ph.D. dissertation, M.I.T.
   1968b   "A comparison of two theories of pronominalization", M.I.T.
Fillmore, C. J.
   1968   "The case for case", in E. Bach and R. Harms (eds.), *Universals in Linguistic Theory* (Holt, Rhinehart and Winston), pp. 1-88.
Fischer, S. D.
   1968   "On cleft sentences and contrastive stress", M.I.T.
Fraser, B.
   1968   "Idioms within a transformational grammar".
Grice, H. P.
   1957   "Meaning", *Philosophical Review*, Vol. 66, pp. 377-88.
   1968   "Utterer's meaning, sentence-meaning and word-meaning", *Foundations of Language* 4, pp. 225-42.
Hall, B.
         See Partee·
Hasegawa, K.
   1968   "The passive construction in English", *Language* 44 pp. 230-43.
Jackendoff, R.
   1967   "An interpretive theory of pronouns and reflexives", M.I.T.
   1968   "An interpretive theory of negation", M.I.T., to appear in *Foundations of Language*.
Katz, J. J.
   1966   *The Philosophy of Language* (Harper and Row).
Katz, J. J. and J. A. Fodor
   1963   "The structure of a semantic theory", *Language* 39, pp. 170-210.
Katz, J. J. and P. Postal
   1964   *An Integrated Theory of Linguistic Description* (M.I.T. Press).
Kraak, A.
   1967   "Presupposition and the analysis of adverbs", M.I.T.
Kuroda, S-Y.
   1965   "Generative Grammatical Studies in the Japanese Language", Ph.D. dissertation, M.I.T.

Lakoff, G.
   1965   "On the nature of syntactic irregularity", Ph.D. dissertation, Harvard University.
   1967   "Pronominalization and the analysis of adverbs", Harvard.
   1968   "Instrumental adverbs and the concept of deep structure", *Foundations of Language* 4, pp. 4-29.
Mates, B.
   1950   "Synonymity", *University of California Publications in Philosophy*, pp. 201-26.
McCawley, J. D.
   1968a "Lexical insertion in a transformational grammar without deep structure", Fourth Regional Meeting, Chicago Linguistic Society, April, 1968, Dept. of Linguistics, University of Chicago.
   1968b "The role of semantics in grammar", in E. Bach and R.T. Harms (eds.) *Universals in Linguistic Theory* (Holt, Rhinehart and Winston), pp. 124-69.
   1970   "Where do noun phrases come from?", in R. Jacobs and P. Rosenbaum (eds.) *Readings in English Transformational Grammar* (Ginn and Co.).
Partee, Barbara Hall
   1965   "Subject and Object in Modern English", Ph.D. dissertation, M.I.T.
   1968   "Negation, conjunction, and quantifiers: syntax vs. semantics", mimeographed, UCLA, presented at the Conference on Mathematical Linguistics, Budapest, September, 1968.
Perlmutter, D. M.
   1968   "Deep and Surface Structure Constraints in Syntax", Ph.D. dissertation, M.I.T.
Quine, W. V.
   1960   *Word and Object* (Wiley and Sons).
Ross, J. R.
   1967   "Constraints on Variables in Syntax", Ph.D. dissertation, M.I.T.
Scheffler, I.
   1955   "On synonymy and indirect discourse", *Philosophy of Science*, pp. 39-44.
Searle, J.
   1968   *Speech Acts: An Essay in the Philosophy of Language* (Cambridge University Press).
Stampe, D. W.
   1968   "Toward a grammar of meaning", *Philosophical Review*, Vol. 78, pp. 137-74.

SOME EMPIRICAL ISSUES IN THE THEORY
OF TRANSFORMATIONAL GRAMMAR*

1.0. The most recent attempt to give a general synthetic view of the theory of transformational grammar was about five years ago, in such books as Katz and Postal (1964) and Chomsky (1965), which summarized and extended much work of the early sixties. Since then, there has been a great proliferation of papers and dissertations, and a flood of underground literature that has kept the mimeograph machines humming. In this work, many new and original ideas have been developed and a great variety of phenomena have been studied, often with quite penetrating analyses. There is an appearance of a considerable diversity of points of view — and to some extent, the appearance is correct. However, I think that the dust is beginning to settle, and that it is now perhaps possible to identify a number of real, empirically significant theoretical questions that have been raised, if not settled, in this work. I also think much of the apparent controversy is notational and terminological — including many issues that appear to be fundamental and have been the subject of heated, even acrimonious dispute. This is unfortunate, because it sidetracks serious work, and because occasionally certain questions of some interest are embedded, sometimes buried in these terminological debates.

1.1. As an example, consider the matter of grammaticalness, certainly a fundamental issue: What does a grammar generate? An answer that has been widely accepted and used is: a grammar generates sentences with structural descriptions. Recently, George Lakoff has made what appears to be a radically new proposal

* I am indebted to Ray Dougherty, Ray Jackendoff, Morris Halle, Jay Keyser, and John Ross for very useful comments.

(Lakoff, 1969a). He suggests that a grammar should not generate sentences in isolation, but rather "pairs, (P,S), consisting of a sentence, S, which is grammatical only relative to the presuppositions of P". He raises the question whether it makes sense to speak of the well-formedness of sentences in isolation, removed from all assumptions about the nature of the world, and argues that competence includes the study of the relationship between a sentence and what it presupposes about the world by way of systematic rules. Knowledge of language must include knowledge of these rules.

For example, consider the sentence (1):

(1)   John called Mary a Republican and then *she* insulted *him*
       (where the italicized words are more heavily stressed).

Lakoff observes that the speaker's judgments as to well-formedness will depend on his beliefs, and he says: "I find [this sentence] perfectly well-formed, though those with other beliefs may disagree". Actually, the situation is still more complicated. Thus the decision as to whether (1) is "well-formed", in this sense, depends also on John's and Mary's beliefs. I can insult someone by attributing to him a property that I think admirable but that he regards as insulting. Similarly, even someone sharing Lakoff's beliefs couldn't insult Barry Goldwater by calling him a Republican.

With this qualification, Lakoff's observation is correct. What follows from it? I think very little. "Well-formedness" is a theoretical term. We are free to define it so that it takes its place within a sensible theory. One terminological proposal — the one I would advocate as the most natural — would be this:

(I)   define "well-formed" so that (1) is well-formed independently
       of the beliefs of John, Mary, or the speaker;

(II)   assign to the semantic component of the grammar the task
       of stipulating that (1) expresses the presupposition that for
       John to call Mary a Republican is for him to insult her.

The relation between (1) and the presupposition of course holds independently of anyone's factual beliefs; it is part of the knowledge of the speaker of English, quite apart from his beliefs, or John's, or Mary's. In general, according to this terminology, the grammar generates sentences and expresses the fact that these sentences carry certain presuppositions. It makes no reference to specific beliefs.

Lakoff's proposal is different: it is to define "well-formed" as a relative concept, and to have the grammar generate pairs (S,P) such that S is well-formed relative to P.

For sentences with presuppositions in this sense, nothing hinges on this terminological decision. All the problems remain exactly where they were, in particular, the problem of characterizing the relation between a sentence and its presupposition. The latter is an interesting question. For the moment, I see nothing more that can be said about this particular case, which is typical of those that Lakoff cites, beyond the unilluminating comment I have just made. What may appear at first sight to be a profound issue dissolves into nothing on analysis, though important questions are nevertheless involved.

1.2. Consider a second example, from the same volume. There Ross (1969a) presents "ten arguments that indicate that auxiliaries and verbs are really both members of the same lexical category, *verb*... [and] two arguments which indicate that they must be main verbs".[1] Ross' argument is that the analysis presented in, say, Chomsky (1957) should be replaced by an analysis with the two features [V] and [Aux], where words such as *read, eat,* etc. are specified as [-Aux] as distinct from *be, have* and the modals which are [+Aux], and [+V] is subcategorized into [±Aux]. Consider, in contrast, the analysis he rejects. There, the symbol V was used for such words as *read, eat,* etc. and the feature v was proposed[2] characterizing V's

---

[1]   Of the latter two, the first deals with German, and the second is based on some general observations about word order by Greenberg. Arguments concerning the German auxiliary bear on English only if one is willing to make some general assumptions about translatability of rules that seem to me unwarranted. Ross argues that Greenberg's data could be explained on the assumption that auxiliaries are main verbs. Evidently, the force of the explanation will depend on the independent evidence for the assumption. In this paper, at least, little is presented.

[2]   It is misleading to put the matter in this way, because the notion "feature" had not been developed for syntax at that time. What was proposed was a

as well as *be, have,* and the modals. Thus Ross' proposal is to replace v by $[+V]$ and V by $[+V, -Aux]$. So far, at least, nothing is at stake except the use of the term "verb": shall we use it to refer to V or to v; i.e., in the new notation, to $[+V, -Aux]$ or to $[+V]$?[3] Again, there is an interesting question involved in what appears here largely as a notational issue. Perhaps there are arguments for deriving auxiliaries, or some auxiliaries, by the rules that generate "true verbs" with their various complements. But it is important to distinguish such arguments, if they exist, from merely notational points.

These examples I have given merely for purposes of illustration. I will turn, in a moment, to more difficult cases.

2.0. I will sketch a framework for discussion that would, I believe, be fairly generally accepted (apart from questions of terminology) by many people working on transformational grammar, and then go on to identify some points of controversy that go beyond terminology, that appear to involve empirical issues. I will also indicate my own views on these issues, at present, and sketch briefly what leads me to them.

2.1. To begin, I will repeat some material from my paper Chomsky (1968b), which was an attempt to do something rather similar. Let us assume given the notion "phrase marker" and the notion "grammatical transformation" as a mapping of phrase markers into phrase markers. We may say, then, that a grammar G generates

---

notational device that would now be interpreted as a feature. I have restated Ross' proposal, treating his category V as a feature $[+V]$. Nothing turns on this in the present connection.

[3] I will not go on here to discuss Ross' specific arguments. I find them unconvincing. To cite just one case, he argues if *have* and *be* are $[+stative]$ (hence verbs) we can account for the fact that they are embedded after *seem* by simply requiring that the latter requires a $[+stative]$ complement. But there is a still simpler way to account for the facts, namely to place no condition at all on *seem:* structures that can be sentences in isolation can be embedded as sentential complements of *seem,* a conclusion which is natural enough if one interprets *seem* semantically as a predicate having a proposition as argument. Point by point, the other arguments seem to me equally inconclusive.

a class K of derivations Σ, where Σ is a sequence of phrase markers:

(2) $G \rightarrow K = \{\Sigma : \Sigma = (P_1, ..., P_n)\}$
       Σ is maximal, in the obvious sense
       $P_i = T\ (P_{i-1})$, by some transformation T of G

The grammar G specifies a set of transformations and various conditions on them, for example, ordering conditions. We may assume that P_n, which we will call the "surface structure", determines the phonetic form of the sentence generated by phonological rules.[4]

Apart from the rules and conditions established in a particular grammar there are general principles that belong to universal grammar: for example, the condition of cyclic ordering; the conditions on application of transformations discussed in various forms in Chomsky (1964a,b,c; 1968a) and Ross (1967); and the various conditions on cyclic and noncyclic transformations suggested by Emonds (1969). Among these are, for example, conditions that preclude extraction of noun phrases from the emphasized positions of *John saw Bill and* TOM, *the fact that* BILL *was here surprised me, John believed the claim that Tom read* THE BOOK, *John saw that picture of* TOM, *John wondered whether Bill had seen* TOM, etc.; conditions relating deep structure representation to the possibility of deletion;[5] and conditions that prevent too wide a variation between deep and surface structures.[6] Such universal restrictions are of critical importance. The gravest defect

---

[4]   The assumption is not uncontroversial, but I will not discuss the matter here. For a strong argument that it is false, see Bresnan (1970).

[5]   For some discussion, see Ross (1967) and Chomsky (1968a), particularly chapter 2 note 11. The first reference to the possibility that history of derivation may be relevant to deletion is in Lees (1960).

[6]   More precisely, "shallow structures", to use a term first suggested by Postal. I use the term here to refer to the structures that appear prior to the application of what Emonds (1969) calls "root transformations". Overlooking details, the term refers to structures that appear prior to the application of the last cycle of transformational rules — i.e., in English, prior to such operations as auxiliary inversion, interpolation of parenthetical expressions, and other operations that do not appear to meet the narrow constraints on cyclic rules (if Emonds' theory is correct).

of the theory of transformational grammar is its enormous latitude and descriptive power. Virtually anything can be expressed as a phrase marker, i.e., a properly parenthesized expression with parenthesized segments assigned to categories. Virtually any imaginable rule can be described in transformational terms. Therefore a critical problem in making transformational grammar a substantive theory with explanatory force is to restrict the category of admissible phrase markers, admissible transformations, and admissible derivations, for example, in the ways just mentioned and perhaps others to which I will return.

2.2. The general point may be worth a slight digression. The fundamental problem of linguistic theory, as I see it at least, is to account for the choice of a particular grammar, given the data available to the language-learner.[7] To account for this inductive leap, linguistic theory must try to characterize a fairly narrow class of grammars that are available to the language learner; it must, in other words, specify the notion "human language" in a narrow and restrictive fashion. A "better theory", then, is one that specifies the class of possible grammars so narrowly that some procedure of choice or evaluation can select a descriptively adequate grammar for each language from this class, within reasonable conditions of time and access to data. Given alternative linguistic theories that meet this condition, we might compare them in terms of general "simplicity" or other metatheoretic notions, but it is unlikely that such considerations will have any more significance within linguistics than they do in any other field. For the moment, the problem is to construct a general theory of language that is so richly structured and so restrictive in the conditions it imposes that, while meeting the condition of descriptive adequacy, it can sufficiently narrow the class of possible grammars so that the problem of choice of grammar (and explanation, in some serious sense) can be approached.

---

[7] Insofar as the concern for discovery procedures can be reformulated in these terms, American structuralism of the 1940's was surely on the right track, in principle — see Chomsky (1968a) for discussion.

Notice that it is often a step forward, then, when linguistic theory becomes more complex, more articulated and refined — a point that has been noted repeatedly (see, for example, Chomsky, 1965, p. 46). For example, it is a step forward when we complicate linguistic theory by distinguishing among all imaginable rules the two categories of "transformational rules" and "phonological rules", with their specific properties, and formulate conditions on their application and interrelation. Similarly, conditions of the sort cited a moment ago complicate linguistic theory and constitute a step forward in that they restrict the class of possible sets of derivations (hence languages) that can be generated by theoretically admissible grammars; i.e., they restrict the choice of K in (2). It can be expected that further progress will come with the discovery of additional formal and substantive universals: a more explicit and detailed articulation of the properties of various parts of grammars, their interrelation, the kinds of rules that can appear in them, and so on.

Given the framework already outlined, it is correct to say that the "most conservative" theory is one that has no more theoretical apparatus than what was described: phrase markers and transformations. The descriptive power of such a system is enormous. Hence this is a rather uninteresting theory. It can be made still more uninteresting by permitting still further latitude, for example, by allowing rules other than transformations that can be used to constrain derivations. This further weakening of the notion "grammar" would permit more grammars and more sets of derivations. Improvements from the worst possible case will come by placing more restrictive conditions on the choice of grammars, limiting the kinds of rules that can appear in them and the ways in which these rules can operate. Permitting a broader class of "derivational constraints" within particular grammars is a step towards a worse theory;[8] but general conditions on the choice of

---

[8] We may, nevertheless, be forced to this regression on empirical grounds, by the discovery that this additional latitude is required for descriptive adequacy.

rules and the way they may apply, no matter how complex and detailed these conditions may be, could be a step towards empirical adequacy, specifically, towards that aspect of empirical adequacy that I have called "explanatory adequacy" (Chomsky, 1964, 1965).

Thus it is misleading to say that a better theory is one with a more limited conceptual structure, and that we prefer the minimal conceptual elaboration, the least theoretical apparatus. Insofar as this notion is comprehensible, it is not in general correct. If enrichment of theoretical apparatus and elaboration of conceptual structure will restrict the class of possible grammars and the class of sets of derivations generated by admissible grammars, then it will be a step forward (assuming it to be consistent with the requirement of descriptive adequacy). It is quite true that the burden of proof is on the person who makes some specific proposal to enrich and complicate the theoretical apparatus. One who takes the more "conservative" stance, maintaining only that a grammar is a set of conditions on derivations, has no burden of proof to bear because he is saying virtually nothing.

Consider, for example, the issue of "autonomous phonemics". Suppose that we have a theory that defines "phonological rule", and "derivation" in the sense of Chomsky and Halle (1968). Suppose further that someone were to propose, as a general condition, that there is a level of representation meeting the conditions of "autonomous phonemics" (i.e., linearity, invariance, and so on, in the sense of Chomsky, 1964; Postal, 1968), and that in every derivation, one step must be a representation in terms of the level of autonomous phonemics. This might be a theoretical advance, in that it limits the class of grammars and the possible sets of derivations, IF it could be shown that no linguistically significant generalizations are lost by placing this additional condition on grammar. (If it could be shown, further, that this additional condition leads to explanation of certain phenomena, then of course it would be additionally confirmed.) It is for this reason that Halle's argument against autonomous phonemics (Halle, 1959) is of such importance: it demonstrates that significant generalizations are indeed lost if we impose this condition on derivations. In the absence of such a demonstration,[9] the advocate of autonomous phonemics would have something of a case, simply because he was offering a way to restrict the class of possible grammars with no loss of descriptive adequacy. Thus in a weak sense, he meets the "burden of proof" simply by imposing a restrictive general condition that does not lose descriptive adequacy. His argument would, in fact, be considerably strengthened if there were some reason to believe that the task of choosing a grammar — that is, taking the inductive leap — is facilitated by this new general condition.[10]

Perfectly analogous general considerations hold in syntax. Suppose, for example, that we discover two categories of transformation, L (lexical) and non-L (non-lexical), with rather different formal properties. Consider the following hypothesis: no linguistically significant generalizations are lost if all transformations of L are applied before any transformation of non-L, in forming derivations. Suppose we complicate linguistic theory by imposing on grammars the condition that all transformations of L apply before any transformation of non-L. This proposal constitutes a potential step forward in that it restricts the class of grammars. It expresses the claim that the hypothesis just cited is an essential, not an accidental property of language. We must ask questions analogous to those appropriate in the case of autonomous phonemics: is the hypothesis correct in the case of particular grammars?; is the class of grammars restricted in a way that facilitates the choice of grammars?; are there further conditions on derivations that can be expressed in terms of the level of representation ("deep structure") defined as the set of phrase markers that appear in derivations after all transformations of L have applied?; is there any further explanatory value to this concept?; and so on.

I will try to show that the status of deep structure, though conceptually somewhat on a par with that of autonomous phonemics (as

---

[9] Or other counter-arguments of the sort discussed in Chomsky (1964), Postal (1968).
[10] To be sure, general metatheoretic considerations of "simplicity" "plausibility", and so on, might count against him, but it must be emphasized that these are so little understood as to be hardly operative.

has been observed, correctly, by McCawley, Postal, and others), differs in a fundamental way in that, in the case of deep structure, the questions just asked receive positive answers, whereas in the case of autonomous phonemics, they do not. My point at the moment is that the question, in both cases, is an empirical one. There is almost nothing to say of any significance on a "methodological" level. One can point out, a priori, that further elaboration of linguistic theory, in both cases, complicates the theory. Although one wants the "simplest" linguistic theory,[11] in some sense that cannot be specified in a useful way, elaborations and complications of linguistic theory are all to the good insofar as they narrow the choice of grammars and the range of admissible languages (i.e., sets of derivations). Thus the hypothesis of general linguistic theory that deep structures exist, in the sense just explained, is on a par, methodologically, with other conditions on the form of grammar (e.g., those of section 2.1). In all of these cases, similar considerations apply.

2.3. Let me now return to the problem of outlining a linguistic theory that has the latitude to meet requirements of descriptive adequacy, but is sufficiently complex, highly articulated, and specific in its constraints so that the problem of explanatory adequacy can at least be placed on the agenda. Suppose that a grammar is of the form outlined in (2) of § 2.1. I have cited a number of restrictive conditions on transformations. The transformations that meet these conditions I will call "nonlexical transformations". In addition, grammars contain "lexical transformations" with very different properties:

---

[11]   One sometimes hears a similar argument put in this way: true, there is no general notion of "simplicity of linguistic theory" to which we can appeal, but surely if we have a theory with a certain range of theoretical apparatus, and another with all of this and more in addition, the first is preferable. This sounds plausible, until one begins to ask how "theoretical apparatus" is measured. Suppose we have a theory stating that grammars contain rules, and a second, more elaborate theory is proposed holding that they have transformational and phonological rules, with their particular properties. There is no doubt which of the two theories is to be preferred, but which has "more theoretical apparatus"?

(3)   a lexical transformation T replaces a subphrase-marker Q
       by a lexical item I

3.0. The minimal framework outlined so far is common to all those
varieties of linguistic theory that I want to discuss here. A number
of specific questions now arise; in particular, the following:

(4)   (A) what is the relation of the lexical to the nonlexical
           transformations?; what is the nature of the lexical items
           and the lexical transformations?
       (B) How is Σ of (2) related to a representation of the
           meaning of the sentence in question, and what is the
           character of semantic representation and the rules that
           relate it to Σ (if any)?
       (C) Are there any further conditions on K of (2) in addition
           to those cited?; specifically, are there "input conditions"
           on the class of phrase markers that appear as P_1 in
           some $\Sigma \varepsilon K$ (given a grammar G)?; are there output
           conditions on the surface structures P_n?; are there
           conditions on intermediate stages of derivations?

3.1. In the paper mentioned earlier (Chomsky, 1968b) I cited three
variants of the general framework for linguistic theory outlined so
far. The first of these I called the "standard theory". It is the theory
developed (in several variants, in fact) in Katz and Postal (1964)
and Chomsky (1965), the most recent attempt at a general synthesis.
Let us consider how questions (A), (B), (C) of (4) are answered in
the standard theory.
    Consider first the questions (A). It is assumed in the standard
theory that all lexical transformations precede all nonlexical transformations. Furthermore, the subphrase-marker Q of (3) is always
a   designated   dummy   symbol   Δ.   Lexical   transformations   are
unordered. Each lexical item is a system of phonological, semantic,
and syntactic features. The syntactic features specify the lexical transformation uniquely. The concept "deep structure" is well-defined:
the deep structure of a derivation $\Sigma = (P_1,...,P_n)$ is the phrase

marker P_i such that for $j \leqslant i$, P_j is formed from P_{j-1} by a lexical transformation, and for $j > i$, P_j is formed by a nonlexical transformation. Since lexical transformations are constrained as just outlined, the deep structure P_i differs from P_1 only in that occurrences of Δ in P_1 are replaced by lexical items. The general form of P_1 is otherwise preserved in the deep structure.

Consider next the questions (B). According to the standard theory, the deep structure, defined as above, completely determines the semantic representation of the sentence. Thus there is a mapping that assigns to the deep structure a "reading" (or a set of readings, in the case of ambiguity) that contains a specification of all of its semantic properties in some universal notation. Various proposals have been made regarding notations for representation of conceptual structures: complex systems of features, case systems, networks of "thematic" relations, notations modelled on familiar logical systems, and so on (see, for example, Katz (1966, 1967), Gruber (1965), Weinreich (1966), McCawley (1968a), Jackendoff (1968), and many others).

Turning next to the questions of (C), the standard theory assumes both "input" conditions" and "output conditions" on K. That is, there are independent conditions on deep structures and surface structures. The conditions on deep structures are determined by base rules: a context-free grammar that generates the initial structures P_1 of (2), and a lexicon which assigns to each lexical item contextual features that permit the item in question to be inserted into P_1, replacing some occurrence of Δ. It is assumed that these base conditions may vary to some extent from language to language, but within certain general limits (for example, it is suggested in Chomsky (1965) that there exists a fixed set of grammatical functions that the rules of the categorial component may determine, and that lexical transformations are restricted to strictly local transformations or to rules that refer to heads of related phrases; in Chomsky (1967), still narrower conditions are suggested).

Furthermore, surface structures must meet certain output conditions. Specifically, it is assumed that there is a designated symbol # which cannot appear internally to a well-formed surface structure.[12] Obligatory transformations can be defined, in some cases at least, in terms of this notation, as discussed in Chomsky (1965).

It is also possible to extend the same notation to the description of certain types of deviance. For example, # may be introduced when some rule is violated in a derivation, indicating that the sentence is not well-formed, though perhaps still interpretable. To mention one example of some interest, consider the matter of violations of constraints on application of transformations. Thus such structures as *what did John believe the claim that John read* (from *John believed the claim that John read something*) or *who did John see the picture of* are formed only by violation of these conditions on application, though *what did John believe that John read* or *who did John see a picture of* are well-formed (see the references of § 2.1. for discussion). Suppose that # is assigned to the category X when a transformation is applied in violation of a constraint on the phrase dominated by X. Then the sentence will be interpretable, as it in fact is, though designated as not well-formed.

That this may be more than a mere notational point is suggested by an interesting observation by Ross (1969b). He argues plausibly that (5) is derived by applying a *wh*-inversion transformation (followed by deletion of *Bill saw*) within the second conjunct (6) of the structure underlying (5):

(5)   he believes that Bill saw someone, but I don't know whom
(6)   I don't know [Bill saw whom].

He observes, however, that such sentences as (7) are well-formed[13],

---

[12]   Similarly, Δ cannot appear in a surface structure. Since # and Δ, as defined, are in complementary distribution, they can be identified. I will not consider here some important studies of output conditions, the results of which must surely be incorporated into syntactic theory. I have in mind what appear to be graded acceptability conditions involving surface form as discussed in Ross (1967) and conditions on word (and perhaps sentence) structure of the sort investigated in Perlmutter (1968).

[13]   Actually, he maintains rather that they are deviant, but less so than (8). The question is not relevant here. What is at issue is only whether in determining (degree of) deviance, we refer to presence of # only in the surface structure or, alternatively, to its presence anywhere in the derivation as a feature of the

although the structure (8), which presumably underlies the second conjunct, is not well-formed:

(7)   he believes their claims about some products, but I don't know which (ones)

(8)   I don't know which products he believes their claims about

These observations would be accounted for by the notational device just proposed. Thus when the *wh*-inversion transformation is applied to form (8), the NP "their claims about" is assigned #, since a general constraint on application of transformations is violated. Accordingly, (8) is interpreted as deviant. But if we go on to form (7) along the lines Ross suggests, the NP is deleted. Thus the derivation is not "filtered out" as deviant by the output condition that # cannot appear internally in a surface structure. Thus (7) is well-formed. The same is true in many other cases: e.g., *he has plans to send some of his children to college, but I don't know which (ones)*, but * *I don't know which children he has plans to send to college;* etc.

The point is of some interest because Ross is led, by these observations, to suggest that some general notion of "derivational constraint" might be needed to account for the facts. Everyone would agree that unless further elaborated, the suggestion that grammars contain "derivational constraints" is vacuous. Any imaginable rule can be described as a "constraint on derivations". The question is: what kinds of rules ("derivational constraints") are needed, if any, beyond those permitted by the standard theory? It is therefore of interest to see that in this case (which is, to my knowledge, the only plausible one that has been discovered in recent work — see below) a very simple and specific device, not unnatural on other grounds, suffices to account for the observed phenomena, so that a trivial modification of the standard theory suffices. The point is important for the reasons already given: the great weakness of the theory of transformational grammar is its enormous descriptive power, and this deficiency becomes more

---

category X that is deleted. Thus the issue is one that belongs to the theory of interpretation of deviant structures.

pronounced to the extent that we permit other rules beyond transformations (i.e., other sorts of "derivational constraints").

3.2. The work of the past few years has revealed quite a few
inadequacies in the standard theory, as just outlined, and much of
the theoretical debate now in progress has to do with attempts to
overcome some of these problems. Two are discussed in Chomsky
(1968b). The first accepts the standard theory approximately as
given, and proposes a few revisions and extensions: I will refer to
this as the "extended standard theory" (henceforth, EST). Referring
to questions (A)-(C) of (4), EST retains the assumptions of the
standard theory with regard to (A) and (C), but modifies the
answers proposed for (B), as follows: semantic interpretation is
held to be determined by the pair (deep structure, surface structure)
of Σ, rather than by the deep structure alone; further, it is proposed
that insofar as grammatical relations play a role in determining
meaning, it is the grammatical relations of the deep structure that
are relevant (as before), but that such matters as scope of "logical
elements" and quantifiers, coreference, focus and certain kinds of
presupposition, and certain other properties, are determined by
rules that take surface structure (more precisely, phonetically
interpreted surface structure) into account. A number of examples
were given there. For much more extensive discussion, along
somewhat similar lines, see Jackendoff (1968).

3.3. An alternative to EST that has been developed quite extensively
in the past two or three years has come to be known as "generative
semantics", and this is the third theory discussed in Chomsky
(1968b). At that time, there was no clear formulation to which one
could refer, but this difficulty has been remedied by the appearance
of Lakoff (1969b,c). Comparison of the alternatives is facilitated
by the fact that these papers adopt, with only a few changes, the
general framework and terminology of Chomsky (1968b), so that
differences between EST and generative semantics, as so conceived,
can be identified with relative ease. Let us consider, then, how
generative semantics deals with the questions (A)-(C) of (4).

With regard to questions (A), this approach interprets the notion of lexical transformation as follows: Q in (3) is a subphrase-marker which expresses the meaning of the item I,[14] and I now contains no semantic features, but only phonological and syntactic features. Furthermore, Lakoff insists that Q contain no lexical items; thus the lexical transformation is a one-step mapping from a notation involving no lexical items into another notation, with a lexical item replacing Q. Furthermore, the requirement that nonlexical transformations precede lexical ones is relaxed; now they may be interspersed freely. Thus in general, the notion "deep structure" is not defined, as it is in the standard and extended standard theory.

Turning now to the questions (B), there are two different versions of generative semantics that have been proposed. Postal (1969a) appears to take the position that the initial phrase marker P_1 of Σ (cf. (2)) can be taken as the semantic representation, as was suggested also by McCawley (1968a). Lakoff, however, takes a rather different position. For him, the semantic representation is a sequence such as (9):

(9)   Semantic representation $= (P_1, PR, Top, F,...)$, where PR is a conjunction of presuppositions, Top is an indication of the 'topic' of the sentence, F is the indication of the focus, and ... indicates other elements of semantic representation that might be needed (Lakoff, 1969b).

Accordingly, a semantic representation is not a phrase-marker at all, and hence is not part of a derivation. Rather, it is a formal object that contains the initial phrase marker P_1 of the derivation Σ, along with much else.[15]

As regards questions (C), generative semantics permits a wide range of conditions on derivations beyond the input and output

---

[14]   This will be sharpened in a moment.

[15]   To be sure, the semantic representation could, trivially, be represented as a phrase marker, e.g., by defining a new symbol σ and forming the phrase-marker $P_1 \sigma PR \sigma Top \sigma F \sigma$ ... (assuming, that is, that PR, Top, F, ..., are represented as phrase markers). As noted earlier, the notion "phrase marker" can accommodate an enormous range of possibilities. I return to this matter below.

constraints of the standard and extended theory. I return to this matter directly.

4.0. Summarizing so far, we have specified a general framework and three specific variants: the standard theory, the extended standard theory, and generative semantics. In my opinion, the standard theory is inadequate and must be modified. The evidence now available seems to me to indicate that it must be modified to the extended standard theory (EST). Furthermore, when some vagueness and faulty formulations are eliminated, I think we can show that generative semantics converges with EST in most respects. There are a few differences, which I will try to identify and discuss, but in most cases I think that the differences are either terminological, or lie in an area where both theories are comparably inexplicit, so that no empirical issue can, at the moment, be formulated. The clearest and probably most important difference between EST and generative semantics has to do with the ordering of lexical and nonlexical transformations. This, in fact, seems to me perhaps the only fairly clear issue with empirical import that distinguishes these theories. My feeling is that present evidence supports the narrower and more restrictive assumption of the (extended) standard theory that nonlexical transformations follow all lexical transformations, so that "deep structure" is a well-defined notion, and so that the conditions on deep structure given by base rules narrowly constrain K (the class of derivations Σ). This, however, is an empirical issue, as distinct from a number of others that seem to me to be terminological, or in an area of indeterminacy and vagueness.

5.0. Before turning to this empirical issue, let me comment briefly on several that seem to me not to be so.

5.1. Lakoff maintains that perhaps the most fundamental innovation of generative semantics is the claim that semantic representations and syntactic phrase-markers are formal objects of the same

kind, and that there exist no projection rules (rules of interpretation) but only grammatical transformations (cf. Lakoff, 1969b,
p. 37). Notice, however, that in his own formulation, a semantic
representation is not a phrase-marker, but rather a sequence
containing a phrase-marker as its first term (see (9) above). However, this is a small point, since as noted (note 15), the semantic
representation can no doubt be reformulated as a phrase marker,
to the extent that its properties are made clear. More generally,
virtually any proposal that has been made concerning semantic
representation can, in equally uninteresting ways, be reformulated
so as to use phrase markers for semantic representation. In
particular, this is surely true of Katz's semantic representations.
It is difficult to imagine any coherent characterization of semantic
content that cannot be translated into some "canonical notation"
modeled on familiar logics, which can in turn be represented with
properly bracketed expressions where the brackets are labeled
(phrase-markers). The whole question is a pseudo-issue. The real
question is whether phrase-markers provide the most "natural" or
the most "illuminating" way to represent semantic content. I cannot
really believe that anyone would be willing to take a stand on this
issue with any conviction, given the present state of descriptive
semantics. In fact, it is quite unclear just what would be the
content of such a claim. Thus this innovation, far from being
fundamental, seems to me nothing more than a terminological
proposal of an extremely unclear sort.

5.2. A second pseudo-issue was discussed briefly in Chomsky
(1968b), but perhaps an additional word of clarification is in order.
It was pointed out earlier that EST differs from the standard theory
only with respect to question (4B), specifically, in its assumption
that surface structures determine certain aspects of semantic interpretation. There is, of course, a trivial way to modify the standard
theory so that it will be compatible with virtually anything that
might be discovered about the relation between surface structure
and semantic interpretation, yet still retaining the condition that
deep structures determine semantic interpretation fully. Suppose,

for example, that focus and presupposition[16] are determined by rules applying to surface structure, call them the rules R. Let us now modify the standard theory so that alongside of the rules of the categorial component (with S as the initial symbol) a grammar may have in addition the rules (10), where f_i and p_j are chosen freely from the categories of formal objects that serve as focus and presupposition, respectively:

(10) $S' \rightarrow S\ f_i\ p_j$

Thus the initial phrase marker P_1 generated by the categorial component of the base will be of the form (11), instead of P_1, as before:

(11)

$$
\begin{array}{ccc}
 & S' & \\
\hline
P_1 & f_i & P_j
\end{array}
$$

Transformations now apply as before, paying no attention to f_i, p_j. Thus instead of $\Sigma = (P_1,...,P_n)$ we have (12):

(12) $\Sigma' = (P_1\ f_i\ p_j,\ P_2\ f_i\ p_j,...,\ P_n\ f_i\ p_j)$,

where each term $P_k\ f_i\ p_j$ is a phrase-marker. Finally, we add an output condition C that accepts Σ' as well-formed just in case P_n, f_i, and p_j are related by the rule R. This revision of the standard theory (call it "version II" of EST) preserves the condition of the standard theory that deep structures alone determine semantic interpretation. Version II differs from the standard theory precisely in that it permits new kinds of output conditions, a greater latitude with respect to question (4C). Of course, the two versions of EST are empirically indistinguishable (in the respect cited).

As noted in Chomsky (1968b), if certain aspects of semantic interpretation are determined from surface structure, then the standard theory must be modified (in either of the two ways just

---

[16]   In one sense; there are several senses that have appeared in the literature, as noted (though inadequately) in Chomsky (1968b).

outlined) and, a fortiori, generative semantics is untenable in the forms in which it had been so far discussed, with P_1 of Σ serving as the semantic representation. Of course, generative semantics could be modified along the lines of version II of EST. This modification is precisely what Lakoff (1969b,c) presents as his formulation of the revised theory of generative semantics. Thus he permits new output conditions (which he calls "derivational constraints") relating semantic representation and surface structure.[17] The only difference is that, in the specific case of focus and presupposition, he chooses the notation (9) instead of (10), taking semantic representation to be a sequence of formal elements rather than a phrase-marker.[18]

There is only one apparent difference between the revised "generative semantics" as based on (9) and the second version of EST formulated in Chomsky (1968b) and just restated; namely (apart from focus, presupposition, etc.), Lakoff assumes that P_1 "is" the semantic representation whereas EST assumes that P_1 "determines" the semantic representation. This apparent difference also seems to fade away under analysis (as we shall see below), leaving only the issue of ordering of various kinds of transformations and perhaps wealth of descriptive devices.

5.3. Putting aside for the moment the apparent difference in how P_1 is viewed, we note that Lakoff's revised generative semantics is simply a notational variant of EST. What leads him, then, to assert that it is an entirely different system? In part, this may result from a misstatement in his presentation of the empirical content of EST (either version). The proposal of EST is that semantic interpretation applies to the pair (deep structure, surface structure), with the qualifications noted above concerning surface structure. In particular, grammatical relations are determined by deep structure, focus and presupposition (in the sense discussed) by surface

[17] Or perhaps shallow structure — cf. note 6.
[18] Inconsistently, as just noted, since elsewhere he states that semantic representations are phrase-markers — indeed, this is held to be the fundamental innovation of generative semantics. Lakoff discusses the notion of focus in (1969c) but incorrectly identifies his version of some remarks of Halliday's with the quite different formulation in Chomsky (1968b).

structure, and certain other aspects of semantic interpretation, such as coreference, by both deep and surface structure. Lakoff asserts that to say that specific aspects of semantic representation (say, focus and presupposition) are determined by principles operating on surface structure is equivalent to "the more neutral locution 'semantic representation and surface structure are related by a system of rules'" (1969c). EST, however, makes a stronger claim: that the relation between surface structure and these specific aspects of semantic representation is independent of other terms in the derivation. This may be right or wrong, but it is quite different from the more neutral locution that Lakoff offers as a paraphrase.

The belief that Lakoff's revised generative semantics (except in the respect that we have put off until later) is a substantive alternative to the formulation of EST that Lakoff paraphrases in his exposition may also be fostered, in part, by some variation in the use of the term "derivational constraint". For Postal (1969a, p. 235) a derivational constraint is a restriction on the sequence of trees which can occur in a well-formed sentential derivation: it is, then, a condition on Σ of (2). This is a natural terminology, given that Σ is called a "derivation". Lakoff does not define "derivation", but he uses the term "derivational constraint" not only for constraints on terms of Σ, but also for any condition relating Σ, or some term of Σ, to some aspect of the semantic representation. For example, he writes that "semantic representation and surface structure are related by a system of ... derivational constraints" (1969b, p. 120). Thus a "derivational constraint" can relate the formal object (9), which is not a phrase-marker, to surface structure, which is a term of a derivation. If Lakoff were to accept the terminological proposal of version II of EST (i.e., with (10)-(12)), his term "derivational constraint" would be synonymous with "constraint on derivation", as presumably intended. In this case, however, it is evident that this version of generative semantics (except for the status of P_1 and the matter of ordering) is compatible with anything that might be discovered about the relation of syntax and semantics. Postal's concept of derivational constraint,

though it enormously increases the descriptive power of transformational grammar, at least may leave some empirical content
to the theory. But in Lakoff's sense, where a "derivational constraint" is any conceivable principle relating some term of a
derivation to another or to some aspect of semantic representation,
it is difficult to see what is excluded by the theory which proposes
that grammars include "derivational constraints". As this theory is
presented, it is not even required that derivational constraints be
pairwise constraints; they are merely conditions that limit the
choice of derivations and semantic representations.

To simplify terminology, I suggest that we replace the term
"derivational constraint" by its equivalent, "rule of grammar".
Then the standard theory asserts that the rules include transformations, the base rules, and the output condition noted, along with
the rules that map deep structures onto semantic representations.
EST identifies certain aspects of semantic representation that are
determined by deep structure, others that are determined by
surface structure, but otherwise permits no new sorts of rules (or in
version II, it allows a new type of output condition in place of rules
relating surface structure and semantic interpretation). Generative
semantics in Postal's sense claims that rules of interpretation of
deep structures can be eliminated in favor of transformations, and
permits other rules of an unspecified sort restricting derivations.
Lakoff goes further, permitting any rule imaginable, so far as I
can see.

Of course, all would agree that the fundamental problem of
linguistic theory is to determine what kinds of rules (derivational
constraints) exist. EST and Lakoff's generative semantics agree that
there are transformations and rules relating surface (or shallow)
structure to certain aspects of semantic representation, and they
agree that there are general conditions on transformations.[19] They

[19] Here too Lakoff's terminology may be misleading. He states that a
transformation is a "local constraint", relating two successive terms of a
derivation, and that general conditions on application such as those mentioned
in § 2.1 are "global constraints". This leads him to the conclusion that "global
constraints" of a much more general kind would be quite natural. However,
the conditions on application are, in fact, not "global constraints" in the

differ with respect to the rules introducing lexical items. Further, Lakoff suggests that many other kinds of rules are necessary. Of course, to say this is not to provide an alternative theory. Rather, any indication that this may be so simply poses a problem, for which a theoretical account is awaited. I return to this matter below.

6.0. Let us consider next the matter of the lexical insertion transformations. Here there appears to be a substantive difference between EST and generative semantics.

6.1. Generative semantics holds that a lexical transformation replaces a subphrase-marker Q by an item I, where I is a set of phonological and syntactic features. Furthermore, it has been proposed (cf. McCawley, 1968b; Morgan, 1969) that Q must be a constituent of the phrase marker. This is almost never the case, it would appear. For example, we must presumably insert *uncle* in place of the subphrase-marker *brother of (mother or father)*, but the latter is no constituent. Rather, underlying the phrase *uncle of Bill*, we would presumably have (*brother of* [(*mother or father*) OF BILL]), where the italicized item is what is replaced by *uncle*. Of course, the italicized item could be made a constituent by a new and otherwise unmotivated rule of "collapsing". This is the approach taken by McCawley in the case of words such as *kill* = "cause to die". In the proposed underlying structure, *John caused Bill to die* (or *John caused Bill to become not alive*), the unit that is replaced by *kill* is not a constituent, but it becomes one by the otherwise quite unnecessary rule of predicate raising. Such a device

---

general sense, but rather conditions that constrain any pair of successive terms of a derivation, i.e., conditions on local constraints.

Though this has no bearing on the present discussion, it should be noted that Lakoff's definition of "transformation" is incorrect. It would not, for example, distinguish between the identity transformation and a permutation of two nodes of the same category; the pair of "tree conditions" (A-B-A, A-A-B) would define two distinct transformations; etc.

will always be available, so that the hypothesis that Q is a constituent has little empirical content.[20]

If we insist that there be a "natural" or a "motivated" rule to make Q a constituent, then the claim that Q is a constituent in a lexical insertion operation seems untenable. Consider, for example, the word *assassinate*, which, in terms of this approach, should replace everything but X in "kill X by unlawful means and with malice aforethought, where X is human, reasonably important,...". There is no way, without extreme artificiality, to make all of this, except for X, a constituent. Yet it is just this that would be required by the assumption that a lexical transformation inserts an item with only phonological and syntactic features for a subphrase-marker Q that is a constituent.

What is true of *assassinate* is true of most words. Consider, for example, the tone of sinister intent that is associated with *cohort* or *henchman* as compared with *colleague;* or consider the many examples analyzed in an illuminating way by Fillmore (1969) in terms of assertion and presupposition. Or compare, say, the word *dissuade* with *persuade not*, where the former, but not the latter presupposes some sort of intention on the part of the person dissuaded — thus you would not speak of dissuading John from standing on the corner or from being optimistic, unless he was

---

[20] Morgan tries to give some further content to this assumption by arguing that rules forming constituents Q for lexical insertion meet the general conditions on application of transformations (cf. § 2.1 above). Thus he claims that there cannot be a verb *sneep* with a meaning such that *John saw Mary laying a wreath at the grave of the unknown hippie* is a paraphrase of *John sneeped Mary laying a wreath at the grave of the unknown*, since these conditions prevent *hippie* from being moved out of this position and attached to *see*. But if this were the reason for the impossibility of *sneep* in this sense, then there should be a possible *John sneeped taking a picture of* meaning *John tried taking a picture of a hippie*, since *hippie* is extractable from this context. The latter, however, is equally bad, so that this argument collapses.

On the relation of *kill* to *cause-to-die*, see Fodor (1969). Notice that the situation with respect to *uncle* is worse than as stated here. If a child were born to a brother-sister marriage, the father would not be its uncle. Laws against incest is no part of the meaning of *uncle*. Therefore Q must contain the information that an uncle is distinct from the father, a fact that requires still more elaborate collapsing rules.

doing so with some particular intent and exercise of will, though you might speak of persuading him not to, in such cases. See also note 20. The point is general, and indicates that condition (3) of § 2.3 can be met by generative semantics only if lexical transformations are operations of a markedly different sort from non-lexical ones. This is not to deny that certain (perhaps all) aspects of meaning can be paraphrased in a canonical notation using phrase-markers, which are then mapped onto phrase-markers with lexical items by "transformations". Given the enormous descriptive power of the concepts "phrase-marker" and "transformation", this thesis can hardly be doubted.

6.2. One might try to retain some substance for the view that lexical items are inserted by transformation in a different way. Suppose that we restrict principle (3) of § 2.3. as follows. Let us distinguish between assertion and presupposition in the case of lexical items, along the lines of Fillmore (1969), and say that the lexical insertion transformation applies in a derivation, replacing a subphrase-marker Q by a lexical item I, where Q represents what is "asserted" by I, but only under the condition that what is presupposed by I is indicated in the semantic representation. This proposal is given by Lakoff (1969c, p. 31). Thus instead of inventing some exotic transformation to insert *assassinate* for its paraphrase, we insert *assassinate* for Q = "killed" (approximately), but only when the presupposition is expressed that the person killed is reasonably important, etc. Recall that the semantic representation, in Lakoff's terms, is a sequence $(P_1, PR,...)$, where PR is a conjunction of presuppositions. Presumably, what is intended is that the presupposition of *assassinate* is one term of this conjunction. Now the lexical insertion transformations can be more restricted, and perhaps one can even preserve the principle that Q is a constituent.

As it stands, this proposal too is untenable. Thus to insert the word *assassinate, criticize, dissuade, accuse,* etc., it is not enough that the presuppositions associated with these words appear as conjuncts of PR, which is one term of the semantic representation. It is necessary, furthermore, to relate the presupposition in question to the position in the phrase-marker which is to be filled by the verb with this presupposition. It is difficult to see how this can be done unless the term PR of the semantic representation virtually duplicates the structure of the phrase-markers that constitute the derivations. For example, if lexical insertion is to take place in an embedded constituent, the presupposition associated with this insertion must be restricted in some way to this position of embedding. Even this elaboration, which is bad enough, would be insufficient if, indeed, lexical insertion can take place at arbitrary stages of derivation, so that there is no way to duplicate in PR the structure of the phrase-markers in which insertion takes place (except by arbitrary coding devices).

Furthermore, it is not at all clear what would now be "meant" by PR. Thus PR is intended to express the presuppositions of the utterance, and it is defined as a conjunction of presuppositions. But it is obvious that the presupposition associated with a lexical item in an embedded sentence need not be a presupposition of the entire sentence.[21] Or, to illustrate some of the difficulties with an oversimplified example, suppose that *accuse NP of Ving* means "state that NP V's" where it is presupposed that it is wrong for NP to V. Then, given the proposal under consideration, the sentence *For John to accuse Bill of lying is worse than for John to state that Bill lied* derives from *For John to state that Bill lied is worse than for John to state that Bill lied*, with the presupposition that John regards it as wrong for Bill to lie, where *accuse* replaces the first occurrence of *state*. Not only is this an unacceptable conclusion in itself, but we must also conclude that the same source underlies the sentence *For John to state that Bill lied is worse than for John to accuse Bill of lying*. There are many similar problems. Somehow, the presupposition must be linked in the underlying "semantic representation" to the specific point in the phrase marker to which it is relevant.

I do not see any way to make sense of this proposal except by

[21] See Langendoen and Savin (1969) for a discussion of the question of how presuppositions of sentences are determined from assertions and presuppositions of embedded structures.

having PR, in some way, reflect the internal structure of the phrase-markers of Σ that are subject to lexical insertion. If, in fact, lexical insertion can take place at any point in Σ, the problem seems utterly hopeless. If lexical insertion were restricted to a particular term of Σ, as in the standard theory, the proposal would be intelligible, but rather pointless. It would amount to duplicating this term of Σ in PR. But quite apart from this, it is merely a play on words to use the term "transformation" for an operation that inserts an item I for a subphrase-marker Q of term P_i of a derivation $\Sigma = (P_1,...,P_n)$, ON THE CONDITION THAT PR (a term of $(P_1, PR,...)$, which is the semantic representation of Σ) CONTAINS A CERTAIN CONJUNCT. Such an operation is radically different in its properties from any non-lexical transformation, even though of course it could be described as a mapping of phrase-markers onto phrase-markers, if we modify Lakoff's theory along the lines of version II of EST (see note 15).

6.3. Once again, it seems that there is no substance to the proposal that lexical insertion is an operation inserting a lexical item for a phrase-marker representing its meaning. No empirical issue is raised by this proposal. There seems no way of avoiding the usual assumption that a lexical entry contains a complex account of conceptual structure, nuance, presuppositions, and so on, and that this account involves grammatically related elements in the sentence. One can no doubt use the notation of phrase-markers and transformations to present this information, but this, if true, merely testifies to the enormous descriptive power of these devices. In any event, these "lexical insertion" transformations bear little resemblance to non-lexical transformations, and no insight is gained by this approach, which seems to raise only terminological issues.

Generative semantics has attempted to incorporate the following two assumptions, regarding lexical insertion operations: (1) each such operation introduces an item I with no intrinsic semantic content; (2) this item I replaces a subphrase-marker. In Lakoff's version, assumption (2) is partially abandoned, only to raise still further problems. It is quite unclear what the content of a workable proposal might be, incorporating some version of the assumptions (1) and (2). In particular, it is difficult to see how such a proposal might differ from the standard theory, with regard to lexical insertion, unless it can be shown that independently motivated transformations precede lexical insertion. The latter question thus appears to be the only relatively clear empirical issue differentiating generative semantics and EST, so far as lexical items are concerned.

6.4.0. Let us consider, then, the question whether all nonlexical transformations follow all lexical transformations, as asserted in the standard (and extended standard) theory, or whether there are reasons for abandoning this hypothesis, and with it, the hypothesis that deep structures exist as a well-defined level of linguistic structure determined by base rules. I know of four lines of argument that have been explored in an attempt to refute this assumption. The first was McCawley's discussion of *respective-respectively* (McCawley, 1968a). He attempted to construct an argument patterned on Halle's refutation of taxonomic (autonomous) phonemics, that is, to discover a generalization that is unformulable if deep structure is assumed to exist as a level of representation in a generative grammar. I am frankly unable to piece together his argument with any certainty, but I think there is no doubt that he did not succeed in constructing such a generalization. And his own positive suggestions seem to reduce merely to a variant of the standard theory.[22]

---

[22] I have discussed this argument in some detail in Chomsky (1968b). Lakoff (1969) claims that the position I tried to reconstruct from McCawley's scattered argument is actually a position that McCawley rejects, rather than the one he proposes. Since Lakoff gives no argument at all for this claim (specifically, no reference to McCawley's text) and does not indicate in what respect my reconstruction, which was based on cited comments from McCawley's text, is inaccurate, I cannot comment on his claim — though it may be correct, for as I noted there explicitly, it is quite difficult to reconstruct McCawley's argument. But the whole matter is irrelevant, since as Lakoff himself admits, "McCawley does not propose a characterization of the necessary operation [i.e., the generalization he claims to be inexpressible, given the assumption of deep structure]. He merely points out that there is a generalization to be stated here, and some such unitary operation is needed to state it." That is, he does not give an argument of the type that Halle presented against taxonomic phonemics, which was precisely my point. Lakoff appears to interpret

A second argument was presented by Lakoff in his interesting discussion of instrumentals (Lakoff, 1968). However, this argument collapses when a wider variety of facts are considered.

These two cases are discussed in Chomsky (1968b), and I'll say no more about them here.

6.4.1. A third argument appears in Lakoff (1969b,c). It has to do with the words *persuade, dissuade*. The entire argument, when analyzed in detail, turns on the following factual claim, and only this. Consider the sentences (13)-(15):

(13)   I persuaded John to date many girls
(14)   I persuaded John not to date many girls
(15)   I dissuaded John from dating many girls.

As Lakoff interprets the facts, sentence (13) can mean *there are many girls that I persuaded John to date;* sentence (14) cannot mean *there are many girls that I persuaded John not to date;* sentence (15) cannot mean *there are many girls that I dissuaded John from dating.* Putting the same point differently, we can say (16) but not (17):

(16)   I persuaded John to date many girls, in particular, Mary, Jane,...
(17)   I dissuaded John from dating many girls, in particular, Mary, Jane,...

Similarly, he regards (17) as not well-formed when *dissuade* is replaced by *keep, prevent, deter*, etc. Judgments about these cases can hardly be very firm, but I see no reason to accept these factual claims. The word *dissuade* does indeed seem to be rather like *prevent, deter, keep*, and other verbs that take *from*-complements,

---

McCawley's argument as an attempt to show that semantic representations must be given in the notation of phrase-markers. Further interpretation of Lakoff's argument, in this respect, is impossible without some explanation of the limitations he believes to exist in the expressive power of phrase-markers, specifically some explanation of his claim that Katz-style semantic representation could not be translated into this notation. This seems to be his central point, but I find it totally obscure, even apart from the inconsistency noted above (note 18).

with respect to the interpretation of a following quantifier. In all cases, the interpretation in question seems to me as acceptable as in the case of verbs such as *persuade*, though I stress again the indecisiveness of the factual judgments. In no case do I see any motivation for assuming that part of the "meaning" is an abstract positive verb (underlying *prevent, keep*, etc.) accompanied by a negative particle. Since these are the only relevant empirical observations cited, I will not pursue the argument based on them.[23]

6.4.2. There is a fourth argument due to Jerry Morgan (1969). He observes that the sentence (18) has two senses when *almost* takes *kill* as scope (and a third, which we can disregard, when it takes *kill John* as scope):

(18)   I almost killed John

The two senses in question are as in (19) and (20), respectively:

(19)   I shot at John and missed him by a hair — I almost killed him
(20)   I wounded John almost mortally — I almost killed him

Morgan argues that we can explain this fact by supposing that underlying *kill* is the phrase-marker *cause to die*,[24] and that one reading of *almost kill* "involves the scope of *almost* being internal to *kill;* i.e., the reading paraphrased by 'I caused John to become almost dead'" (i.e., (20)). He claims further that these two readings of *kill John* are differentiated more explicitly in (21), (22):

(21)   what I did was almost kill John
(22)   what I did to John was almost kill him

His point, I believe, is that (22) has the interpretation of (20), whereas (21) has the interpretation of (19). To me it seems, rather,

---

[23]   Lakoff seems to me in error in his assertion that *dissuade* is synonymous with *persuade not*, for reasons noted earlier (p. 143). The presuppositions differ. This question, however, is not material to the argument, since he assumes that lexical insertion requires reference to presuppositions — see section 6.2, above.

[24]   He suggests the "deeper" source *cause to become not alive*, but this has no bearing on the present argument.

that (21) is ambiguous as between (19) and (20), and that (22), as he holds, has the reading of (20). But this, if true, would hardly support his theory, since on his assumptions it should follow that (22) is also ambiguous.

Quite apart from this, there are further difficulties. The range of meaning he perceives seems to be characteristic of many, perhaps all verbs that specify a process that can reach a terminal point: e.g., *I almost solved the problem, I almost persuaded Bill to leave, The planes almost destroyed the city*, etc. The latter, for example, might be interpreted along the lines of (19) or (20). Furthermore, *what the planes did was almost destroy the city* parallels (21) in interpretation, while *what the planes did to the city was almost destroy it* has, as its natural interpretation, the analogue to (20). Yet in this case, there is little sense to the idea of an internal analysis, and surely no causative analysis. Again, the factual judgments seem to me insecure, but so far as they are clear at all, it seems that the whole matter simply has to do with verbs of process with a terminal point. One might, further, speculate that this is a universal charac- teristic of such verbs, and hence not to be described in a particular grammar. In any event, I see no argument here for the assumption that such verbs as *kill* must be introduced by transformations replacing phrase-markers such as *cause-to-die*.

Other difficulties in such an approach have already been discussed (see pp. 142-145). Fodor (1969) presents several arguments in support of a much stronger assertion, namely that the causative analysis is not only unmotivated but in fact unacceptable. His conclusion is approximately what Jackendoff (1969) formulates as the "extended lexical hypothesis", namely, that "the only changes transformations can make to lexical items is to add inflectional affixes such as number, gender, case, person, and tense". Another line of argument leading to the same conclusion has been explored by Joan Bresnan (1970). She suggests that the rules of the phonological cycle apply not to surface structures, as supposed heretofore, but in the course of the transformational cycle. It would follow that either the extended lexical hypothesis is accepted, or else fairly radical modifications have to be introduced in the principles of the phonological cycle. I will not go into these questions here. My own guess is that the extended lexical hypothesis is probably correct, in essence.

6.4.3. There have been a number of other attempts, some quite detailed, to show that certain lexical items must be introduced after certain transformations. To be at all convincing, such an argument against the standard (or extended standard) theory must show that some SYNTACTICALLY MOTIVATED transformation precedes the operation of lexical insertion — that is, some transformation motivated independently of the expression of the meanings of lexical items. As already noted, it will in general be quite difficult to distinguish between rules of semantic interpretation for lexical items and transformations that introduce such items in place of certain phrase-markers in a distinct "semantic" notation. Lakoff (1969c) discusses quite a number of such attempts. I will not try to review them all in detail, but will discuss only the case which he appears to regard as the strongest of the group.

Consider the word *remind*, as in the sentence (23):[25]

(23)   John reminds me of a gorilla

The proposal is that the underlying structure is, approximately, (24):

(24)   I [perceive]$_V$ [John is similar a gorilla]$_S$

Subject-raising and a permutation rule ("Psych-movement") give (25):

(25)   John [perceive]$_V$ me [similar a gorilla]$_S$

Predicate raising produces the phrase [perceive similar]$_V$ which is replaced by *remind*, by a lexical insertion transformation.

The first question to be asked is whether these transformations

---

[25] Lakoff's argument follows Postal (1969b). As far as I can judge, Lakoff correctly extracts the essence of the argument. Postal presents much further evidence which I will not discuss. It seems to me less strong than that which Lakoff presents, involving rather questionable judgments and many interesting, but inconclusive observations. For further discussion see J. Kimball (1969), Bowers (1970), Katz (forthcoming).

are syntactically motivated. Predicate-raising surely is not; it is simply a device to convert phrases that are to be replaced by a lexical item into a single constituent. Though the matter is not relevant here, I might mention that the permutation rule that gives (25) as well as subject-raising seem to me to be at best dubious rules. However, I will not pursue the issue here, because even if these rules are assumed, the case for lexical insertion after they apply seems to me extremely weak.

Lakoff asks, correctly, whether there is any syntactic evidence for the transformational derivation of (23) from (24). He offers the following evidence. Consider the sentences (26):

(26)   to shave oneself is to torture oneself (is like torturing oneself).

The rule that forms such sentences applies freely if the subject is the impersonal, but is restricted in other cases. Thus we cannot have (27) or (28), although (29) is grammatical:

(27)   to shave himself is to torture himself (is like torturing himself)

(28)   Mary says that Bill thinks that shaving herself is torturing herself

(29)   Bill says that to shave himself is to torture himself.

The generalization he suggests is that the rule can apply "when the clause where the deletion takes place is a complement of a verb of saying or thinking and when the NPs to be deleted are coreferential to the subject of that verb of saying or thinking". This principle would permit (29), while excluding (27) and (28).

Suppose, now, that (24) underlies (23), and that the rule in question applies to the underlying form (24). Then from (30) we will derive (31) which becomes ultimately (32):

(30)   John perceive [shaving him similar torturing him]
(31)   John perceive [shaving himself similar torturing himself]
(32)   shaving himself reminds John of torturing himself

However, the principle just formulated will exclude (33):

(33) Mary says that shaving herself reminds John of torturing
      herself

These conclusions are correct: (32) is grammatical but not (33).
Therefore, Lakoff concludes, there is independent syntactic evidence
for the proposed derivation of *remind*, because the transformational
rule that gives (31) must precede lexical insertion.

The argument collapses, however, when one observes that the
formulated principle (quoted above) is inadequate. Thus alongside
of (32) we have such sentences as (34):

(34)   (i) shaving himself seems to John like torturing himself
       (ii) shaving himself makes John think of torturing himself
      (iii) shaving himself brings to John's mind the idea of
            torturing himself
       (iv) shaving himself appears to John to be as pointless as
            torturing himself

One would hardly argue that these derive from something like (30).
Rather these sentences are formally analogous to (32) and indicate
that the rule in question can apply quite freely to such structures,
independently of their postulated transformational source (quite
different, in these cases). In short, the rule in question, whatever it
may be, gives no support to the analysis of *remind*, since it appears
to apply to structures such as (34) which contain no verb of saying
or thinking in the required position.

In fact, the situation is worse. Compare the set (35):

(35)   (i) John reminds me of a gorilla
       (ii) John's presence reminds me of an appointment I missed
            (Mary's diamond ring reminds me of my poverty, etc.)
      (iii) John reminded me of an appointment I missed

Sentence (35i), according to Postal's analysis, derives from something like (24). Sentences (35ii), (35iii) derive from entirely different
sources. It is merely an accident, from this point of view, that they
share the same surface form. Furthermore, one cannot argue that
some "output condition" on surface (or shallow) structure requires

this similarity of form for the various cases of *remind*, since the regularity illustrated in (35) is stateable only prior to transformational rules (such as passive) that yield surface (or shallow) structures. In fact, it is a regularity stateable precisely at the level of deep structure in the sense of the (extended) standard theory.

Furthermore, exactly the same range of interpretations is possible when we replace *remind* in (35) by other phrases such as *make [Bill] think of, bring to [Bill's] mind*, etc. Hence from this point of view there is a double accident: first, in the case of *remind* there is a single syntactic form (stateable at the level of deep structure, but nowhere else) with a range of interpretations corresponding to totally different "underlying" structures; second, other phrases similar in meaning to *remind* share the same range of interpretation, with a fixed syntactic form (stateable only at the level of deep structure).

These observations suggest that *remind* is inserted at the level of deep structure and that the range of interpretation of *remind* (as well as the other phrases similar to it in meaning) is determined by general principles operating at this level of representation. The optimal solution, of course, would be the discovery of general rules, not restricted to the case of *remind*, that express the range of meaning noted without the ad hoc assumption that separate (and presumably unrelated) lexical entries are involved in the set (35) (as well as in the parallel sets involving phrases similar in meaning). To discover such principles is not a trivial matter. Several lines of investigation suggest themselves. Thus the distinction between (35iii) and (35ii) seems analogous to the distinction between *John opened the door* and *the key opened the door* (or to the ambiguity of *John broke the window* — i.e., he did it as an agent or as an object thrown through the window). Perhaps it follows, then, from the principle that an animate subject of a verb of action can be interpreted as an agent. Furthermore, as Jackendoff notes (personal communication), the relation between (35i) and (35ii) seems analogous to that holding between *John irritates me* and *John's presence irritates me*. Perhaps, then, (35i) can be regarded as a special case of (35ii) in sentences with a generic interpretation where the specific characteristic noted explicitly in (35ii) (namely, John's presence, Mary's diamond ring) is not mentioned. It remains to formulate such a principle precisely and to relate it to the principle involved in interpreting animate subjects as agents. Such an approach, if feasible, has the considerable advantage that it would overcome the double anomaly that is otherwise left unresolved.

In short, properties of *remind* seem to provide no support for relaxing the condition of the (extended) standard theory that lexical insertion precedes all rules of the transformational cycle. On the contrary this hypothesis seems to provide the best hope of explaining the properties of *remind* and other phrases with a similar meaning. I know of no other example that suggests a contrary conclusion.[26]

6.5.0. I have mentioned several lines of argument that might yield counter-evidence to the assumption that lexical insertion operations precede all non-lexical transformations. None of them, at the moment, seems to provide any such evidence. Although the possibility obviously cannot be ruled out that such evidence will be

[26] Lakoff mentions one argument (attributed to D. Perlmutter) which he claims "seems to provide clear and incontrovertible evidence" that lexical insertion must follow certain transformations. In Spanish, we have normal noun-adjective agreement in *Mi madre y mi padre son respectivamente alta y bajo* 'my mother and my father are tall (fem.sg.) and short (masc.sg.) respectively'. He claims that in certain dialects the corresponding form with *padres* 'parents' would be *Mis padres son respectivamente alta y bajo* 'my parents are tall (fem.sg.) and short (masc.sg.) respectively'. He concludes, therefore, that the rule inserting *padres* for *madre y padre* must follow the transformational rule of adjective-noun agreement.

The argument is based on the assumption that such *respectively*-constructions are derived by transformation from conjunctions, e.g., the above from *mi madre es alta y mi padre es bajo*. This assumption, however, seems untenable. Consider, for example, the problem of deriving in this way: *the successive descendants of my fruit fly will be heavier, respectively, than the successive descendants of yours*, or any case involving an infinite set or finite set of unknown size. Many other arguments are given in Dougherty (1968, 1970). Thus the gender assignments noted by Lakoff are not explained in his terms in any event. If his empirical observations are accurate, it would appear that gender agreement may be a matter of surface interpretation, perhaps similar to determination of coreference. This would seem not unnatural.

discovered, it seems to me that what evidence is now available supports the more restrictive (and therefore preferable) assumption of the standard theory that lexical insertion operations belong to the base, and that deep structures therefore exist as a significant linguistic level.

In discussing autonomous (taxonomic) phonemics, I noted that the observation that no generalizations are lost if rules are ordered so that such a level appears in derivations would, if correct, be an argument for the existence of this level. The hypothesis, then, would be that this is an essential, not merely accidental property of human languages. As Halle showed, this argument fails in the case of autonomous phonemics, but there seems, at the moment, no reason to doubt that the analogous argument is correct in the case of deep structure. A still stronger argument for autonomous phonemics would be that certain generalizations and limiting conditions on derivations can be formulated in terms of the postulated level. In the case of deep structure, there is good reason to believe that this stronger argument also holds.

6.5.1. I have already noted one example, namely, the case of *remind*. In general, it seems to be true that the properties of lexical items are formulable in terms of a set of phrase markers that are defined by the categorial rules of the base. If true, this is a remarkable fact, expressed as a fundamental principle in the (extended) standard theory. To my knowledge, the principle is well supported by the available evidence, though there is no a priori reason why languages should be so constructed.

6.5.2. There are many other considerations that lead to the same conclusion. One simple example is noted by Jackendoff (1969). Consider the sentences (36):

(36)   (i) a beaver builds dams
         (ii) that beaver builds dams
         (iii) a beaver is building a dam
         (iv) the fattest beaver is the builder

The first sentence can be interpreted only as generic, the second and the third only as specific, while the fourth is ambiguous as between the two interpretations. Clearly, the possibility of generic or specific interpretation is not determined simply by the choice of subject or the choice of predicate, but in part by an interaction between the two. At the level of deep structure, there is a very simple generalization governing such sentences as (36): any noun phrase can be followed by any verb phrase.[27] But the semantic representations will vary with respect to such properties as generic-specific. Thus such sentences as (36) will have varied paraphrases, and if it is supposed that something like the correct paraphrase is the initial term of the derivation, it will merely be a curious accident that at a certain stage of derivation, namely that illustrated by (36), there is the simple generalization just noted. It would, in other words, be claimed implicitly that the grammar of English would be no more complex if this (accidental) regularity did not hold true.

Furthermore, as Jackendoff notes, a theory that somehow derives such forms as (36) from their semantic representations would not only not be able to express the syntactic regularity of such forms, but it will in fact have to rule out the simplest underlying structures for at least some of them. Thus (36iv) will have two quite different initial phrase-markers in its two derivations, one of them similar to the initial phrase-marker of (36i) and the other similar to the initial phrase-marker of (36ii, iii). By accident, later transformations happen to give the forms satisfying the simple regularity illustrated by (36). In addition, it is necessary to ensure that (36i) does not have an initial phrase-marker similar to those of (36ii, iii). If, say, the latter have the underlying form NP-VP, then rules must be added to guarantee that there is no such form that will lead, by transformation, to (36i).

[27] Obviously, this is only a first approximation and further refinements are necessary. Thus certain phrases, for example *any beaver with teeth*, can appear only with one interpretation. This fact is irrelevant to the point at issue, since it requires comparable qualifications in both of the approaches being compared. If we choose to preserve the simplest syntax, with free choice of subject and predicate, the deviance of *any beaver with teeth is building a dam* (etc.) would be attributed to the filtering effect of the semantic rules.

Compare this observation with Halle's argument with respect to autonomous phonemics. Halle showed that some generalization is not formulable IF autonomous phonemics exists as a well-defined level of derivation. Jackendoff's argument indicates[28] that some generalization is not formulable UNLESS deep structure exists as a well-defined level of derivation — furthermore, a level generated independently by base rules.[29]

6.5.3. As a second, more intricate example of a similar sort, consider English derived nominals.[30] These vary widely in interpretation, but are severely constrained in form, in several ways.

First, derived nominals correspond only to forms that exist prior to syntactically motivated transformations. Thus we have such forms as (37) but not (38):

(37)   (i)   John's certainty that Bill will leave
        (ii)   John's eagerness to please
        (iii) the gift of the book to Mary
        (iv)   the belief that John was killed
        (v)   John's surprise at Bill's antics
(38)   (i)   John's certainty to leave
        (ii)   John's easiness to please
        (iii) the gift of Mary the book
        (iv)   the belief of John to have been killed
        (v)   Bill's antics surprise of John.[31]

[28] To prove the point it would be necessary to demonstrate that there does not exist a way to capture the relevant generalization within the alternative framework. The formulations are, for the moment, too loose to permit a demonstration of any such proposition.

[29] Jackendoff's point is strengthened by the observation that determination of such properties as generic-specific seems to depend in part on late, perhaps surface structure (consider, e.g., such examples as *John is hunting a tiger*, *there is a tiger that John is hunting*; *John writes poems, there are poems that John writes*, etc.). Notice also that the regularity exhibited by (36) cannot be a matter of "output conditions" on surface or shallow structures, even if such conditions exist, since it holds only prior to the application of such transformations as passive — i.e., it holds of deep structures.

[30] For detailed discussion, see Chomsky (1967).

[31] Case (v) presupposes that *John is surprised at Bill's antics* is, in effect, involved in the structure underlying *Bill's antics surprise John*. For discussion,

Notice that the proper generalization concerning admissible derived nominals is expressed in terms of deep structure — i.e., the level prior to application of syntactically motivated transformations — a fact that provides evidence for the existence of this level of representation.

Secondly, the patterns in question must exist independently for noun phrases, quite apart from these nominalizations, as we see from such expressions as *the story of Bill's exploits, the message from John to Bill about money, a war of aggression against England, the secretary-general of the UN, his advantage over his rivals, his habit of interrupting, the prospects for peace, prolegomena to any future metaphysics, my candidate for a trip to the moon, a nation of shopkeepers,* and many others.

Thirdly, these forms fall under a simple phrase structure schema that applies as well to verb and adjective phrases, which appear with approximately the same complement structure as nouns.

Fourth, derived nominals have the internal structure of noun phrases — that is, many of them pluralize and take determiners and internal adjectives *(John's several proofs of the theorem, John's uncanny resemblance to Bill, the remarkable proof of the theorem that John presented,* etc.).

Fifth, derived nominals do not contain elements that are unique to verb phrases and never appear in other noun phrases, specifically, aspect. There is, in other words, no derived nominal containing perfect or progressive.

---

see Chomsky (1967), where it is suggested that the latter is a causative of the former. An apparent counter-example to the generalization just formulated is that there are nominals such as *the destruction of the city by the enemy* and *the city's destruction by the enemy* that correspond to passives. However, there are good independent reasons to suppose that the passive is applied to the nominal rather than nominalization being applied to the passive, in such cases. See again Chomsky (1967) for discussion. As noted there, the two components of the passive transformation apply to noun phrases independently of whether these noun phrases correspond to sentences (are nominalizations). Emonds (1969) gives a motivated explanation for the fact that in the case of the nominal, either one or both of the two components of the passive transformation may apply, whereas in the case of sentences, both must apply. Thus there is no passive sentence corresponding to *the destruction of the city by the enemy.*

In all these respects derived nominals differ from gerundive nominals such as *John's refusing the offer*. These are not subject to the wide-ranging, often idiosyncratic variation of meaning that is characteristic of derived nominals; rather, all are related in meaning to the corresponding sentence by simple and uniform principles. As far as form is concerned, gerundive nominals correspond not only to base structures but to derived structures as well *(John's being certain to leave*, etc.); they do not correspond in form to independently existing noun phrases; their forms do not fall under a more general phrase structure schema governing all lexical categories; they do not have the internal structure of noun phrases (* *the refusing the offer*, * *John's sudden refusing the offer*, * *John's provings the theorem); and* they may contain aspect (e.g., *John's having refused the offer).*

The properties of gerundive nominals follow directly from the assumption that there is a transformational process of gerundive nominalization. The very different cluster of properties of derived nominals follows directly from the assumption that they are not transformationally derived, but rather that the base component of the grammar contains a phrase structure schema that applies to all lexical categories (i.e., noun, verb and adjective), and that certain lexical items may appear in more than one lexical category.[32] These

---

[32] For details, see again Chomsky (1967). It is suggested there that there may be still more general similarities in the internal structure of noun phrase, verb phrase, and adjective phrase, reflected in higher order schemata. Interesting arguments in support of this speculation are presented by Bowers (1968, 1969), Selkirk (1970), who point out syntactic relations between qualifiers of adjectives and determiners of nouns (specifiers, in the terminology of Chomsky, 1967). There are also certain semantic similarities among specifiers. For example, the generic-specific property of sentences is partially determined by choice of determiners and verbal auxiliaries (specifiers of nouns and verbs, respectively, in this framework), and it has often been noted that tense systems share certain of the referential functions of determiners — see, for example, McCawley's discussion (1969c) of respects in which auxiliaries have a quantifier-like structure.

If these proposals stand, we can formulate an abstract condition on the base component of any grammar, namely, that it generate structures which, in a well-defined sense, are projected from the basic lexical categories N,V,A, with only certain variation possible (e.g., in range of complements, in order of elements). Furthermore, there is reason to believe that each of these lexical categories is to be taken as a bundle of syntactic features (two features would

assumptions account for the observed convergence of formal properties — that is, the fact that derived nominals have one set of properties and gerundive nominals an entirely different set. Of critical importance, in the present connection, is the fact that the explanation for the convergence of properties in the case of derived nominals depends on the assumption that deep structures exist — the appropriate explanatory principle is formulated in terms of the properties of base structures. If, on the other hand, we were to suppose that each nominal, gerundive or derived, is generated from an initial phrase-marker representing its semantic interpretation, we would fail entirely to explain why the gerundive nominals, with a regular semantic relation to the associated sentence, have the formal properties of sentences, whereas the derived nominals, which would have a variety of different sources, exhibit the convergence of formal properties just noted (i.e., in essence, the properties of noun phrases), differing from gerundive nominals in this respect. All of this would be simply a remarkable accident, from this point of view. The convergence of formal properties and the relation between range of meaning and correspondence to either noun phrase (in the case of derived nominals) or sentence (in the case of gerundive nominals) cannot be explained in terms of universal semantics or properties of transformations — the only devices available to generative semantics for expressing regularities at early stages of derivation — though it can be explained immediately in terms of some general conditions on deep structures. Notice that the failure is one of explanatory, not descriptive adequacy. There is no doubt that the facts noted can be described in a grammar that derives all of these forms by transformation.

This problem has been noted by Lakoff (1969c). He suggests that the regularities noted "are instances of constraints on shallow or surface structure". As in the other cases discussed here, this proposal is untenable, since these regularities do not appear at the level

---

provide the categories: N, V, A, everything else, where N and A share a feature, and V and A share a feature). It seems plausible that such abstract conditions form part of universal grammar, and that they determine the range of potential variation in base structures.

of shallow or surface structure, but only at a more "abstract" level prior to the application of the syntactically motivated transformations, which destroy these regularities. There seems no way to avoid the conclusion that the class K of admissible derivations (cf. (2)) is defined, in part, by categorial rules of the base (phrase structure schemata and context-free phrase structure rules) that restrict the class of initial phrase-markers of derivations. Deep structures, then, are the structures formed from these by insertion of lexical items.[33]

Summarizing, I believe that these considerations again provide strong evidence in support of the (extended) standard theory, with its assumption that deep structures exist as a well-defined level with the properties expressed by base rules.

6.6.0. At this point, I would like to comment on arguments that have been offered against the analysis of derived nominals just reviewed — what I have called the "lexicalist hypothesis". I know of three that have appeared in print.

6.6.1. Ross (1969b) argues as follows. Consider such sentences as (39):

(39)   Bill mentioned his plans to do away with someone, but he didn't mention whom

He argues that the source for the second conjunct must be (40):

(40)   Bill didn't mention whom he plans to do away with.

He concludes that this "provides evidence against any theory of grammar in which 'his plans to do away with someone' is not identical, at some stage, to 'he plans to do away with someone'". But the lexicalist hypothesis denies that these two are identical at any stage of derivation. Consequently, the argument provides evidence against the lexicalist hypothesis.

---

[33] And leading to surface structures meeting the output condition of (4C). It should be noted that there is no evidence that there exist output conditions of the sort presupposed by Lakoff's suggestion. Hence even if, contrary to fact, it were tenable, it would require new and otherwise unmotivated syntactic devices.

Suppose that Ross' argument were valid. Now replace *his plans* in (39) by any of the following: *his plan, those plans of his, his several weird plans*, etc. By the same argument, it follows that all of the resulting phrases (41) must be identical, at some stage of derivation, to *he plans to do away with someone.*

(41) Bill mentioned his plans (his plan, those plans of his, his several weird plans, etc.) to do away with someone.

Therefore the various sentences of (41) must be identical with one another at some stage of derivation. Then either they are synonymous, if they are identical at the initial stage of derivation, or they may be different in initial phrase-marker, different in final structure, but all identical at some intermediate stage D. The question would then arise how the subderivations from initial phrase-marker to D are properly paired with their continuations to surface structure. Without pursuing the matter, I think it is sufficiently clear that in either case, we have reached an intolerable conclusion. Consequently, the argument is at best suspect — and, in fact, it is unclear what force it had even apart from these unacceptable consequences.

6.6.2. Ross presents a second argument against the lexicalist hypothesis in Ross (1968). Here he considers the following expressions:

(42)   his shrug of displeasure
(43)   he shrugged his displeasure
(44)   he-showed (manifested)-his displeasure-by shrugging

He argues that (44) is converted to (43) by an operation that replaces the second term by the fourth, so that the nominalization (42) corresponds to a transform (43), contrary to the lexicalist hypothesis which requires that derived nominals correspond only to base forms.

This argument is extremely weak, even if we accept the idea that something like (44) underlies (43). Notice that *shrugging* in (44) can be replaced by many noun phrases (e.g., *an obscene gesture, an angry letter, a shrug*). Consequently we could accept the hypothesis that the noun *shrug* is a lexical item, and derive both (42) and (43) by an operation that applies to a noun phrase or a sentence of the form (45), replacing the second term by the fourth:

(45)   [he — manifest(ation) — his displeasure — by $\left\{\begin{array}{l} \text{a gesture} \\ \text{shrugging} \\ \text{a shrug} \end{array}\right\}$]

But even this much is dubious, and I question, therefore, that this is at all the correct approach. Consider the sentence (46):

(46)   he manifested his displeasure by a shrug of annoyance (displeasure)

If we assume a rule giving (43) from (44), the structure underlying (46) must be something like *he manifested his displeasure by manifesting his annoyance (displeasure) with a shrug (by shrugging)*. But this seems to give the wrong meaning: he didn't manifest his displeasure by manifesting some emotion, but by a shrug. In any event, the motivation for any such rule is extremely weak. One might just as well propose that all lexical items with some feature (call it [+manifestable]) can appear as nouns in the fourth position of (45) and as head noun or verb in (42)-(43), dispensing with all of these transformations, and the attendant problems.

6.6.3. The only other argument that I know of appears in Postal (1969). He considers the phrase (47) and notes that in it, *America* must be understood as the subject of *attack*.

(47)   America's attempt to attack Cuba

This observation, he claims, is a counterargument to the lexicalist hypothesis since if "such nominalizations are not transformationally derived ... [then] ... no general account of which NP controls complement subject deletion will be possible". The point is that in (48), we can say that the subject, *America*, controls complement subject deletion, but in (49), underlying (47) by the lexicalist hypothesis, some entirely different rule would be needed:

(48)   [America — attempts [America attacks Cuba]s]s
(49)   [America's — attempt [America attacks Cuba]s]NP

The appropriate generalization requires that we assign the same grammatical relation to the pair *(America, attempt)* in (48) and (49) (namely, *America* is subject of *attempt* in both cases). Then we could formulate the principle that the NP that controls complement subject deletion "must be the subject of the immediately dominating clause" (or in these terms, the immediately dominating S or NP).

Postal's counterargument is based on a misunderstanding. He overlooks the essential claim of the lexicalist hypothesis, namely, that grammatical relations must be generalized in such a way that the subject-verb relation holds of *(America, attempt)* in (49), as in (48), and perhaps even of the same pair in the phrase *the American attempt* (where *American* is what Postal calls a Proper-pseudo-adjective (PPA)).[34] Hence nothing follows from Postal's observations, so far as the lexicalist hypothesis is concerned.

6.6.4. These are the only counterarguments that have been suggested in print, to my knowledge, to the lexicalist hypothesis.[35] Since the evidence for the hypothesis is quite strong, I think we must conclude, tentatively, that the hypothesis is well-supported, and consequently, that the assumptions of the (extended) standard theory with regard to deep structure are well-supported as well.

6.6.5. Before turning to the next matter, let us pursue somewhat further Postal's discussion of PPA's, although this is not strictly relevant to the discussion here. He considers such phrases as (50),

[34] See Chomsky (1967) for discussion. PPA's are not discussed there, but the necessary extension is fairly clear. The generalization of grammatical relations is necessary quite apart from the question of control of complement subject deletion, as is the assumption that NP and S function as the domain of transformations. Observe that trivial modifications are required in the rule of complement subject deletion, under this analysis.
[35] Others have been proposed orally, but I know of none that have any force, and since they have not been presented publicly, I will not take the time to discuss them.

arguing that they must derive from the corresponding phrases of (51):

(50)   (i) the American attack on Colombia
       (ii) the Markovian solution of that problem
      (iii) the Persian application for membership
       (iv) the American attempt to attack Cuba
        (v) scholarly attempts to uncover the causes
       (vi) sociological studies
(51)   (i) America's attack on Colombia
       (ii) Markov's solution of that problem
      (iii) Persia's application for membership
       (iv) America's attempt to attack Cuba
        (v) attempts by scholars to uncover the causes
       (vi) studies by sociologists

He argues that the paired phrases share grammatical and selectional relations, conditions on control, and deep structure constraints. Consequently, he concludes that (50) derive from (51).

The argument presented seems to me weak, however. The existence of these similarities is not in doubt, but they can be accounted for exactly as well by a lexicalist approach to PPA's which generalizes the subject-verb relation in the manner just noted and attributes the shared properties to the subject-verb relation itself, along the lines discussed in Chomsky (1967). Hence the facts that Postal presents seem to me to be quite neutral as between the assumption that (50) derive from (51) and the assumption that all are (essentially) base forms.

However, looking into the matter further, I think there is a good argument that the PPA's not only NEED not derive by transformation, but in fact that they DO not. In fact, PPA's share some of the properties of derived nominals that argue against a transformational derivation, in particular, their semantic idiosyncrasy.[36] Thus

---

[36] This characteristic argues against the transformational derivation for reasons noted earlier in connection with derived nominals. That is, on the latter assumption it would merely be an accident that the PPA constructions share formal properties stateable by simple phrase structure constraints, given that they arise by transformation from very different sources. On the other hand, the

Postal's examples would be consistent with the transformational derivation of (50) from (51) that he proposes only if the paired phrases were synonymous.[37] This, however, is not the case. For example, the phrase *the Markovian solution* does not mean *Markov's solution* (cf. (50ii)-(51ii)). If I say that this problem has no Markovian solution, I mean that it has no solution along Markovian lines, not that it has no solution by Markov. The same is true in general of such phrases as *a Markovian analysis, a Fregean analysis*, etc. Similarly, the pairs (50v)-(51v) are surely not synonymous (consider: *the most scholarly attempts to uncover the causes were made by journalists*). A similar discrepancy appears in (50vi)-(51vi) (consider: *the best sociological studies are by anthropologists*). Other problems arise in the case of (i), (iii), (iv) of (50)-(51). Thus (50iii) seems quite analogous in form and meaning to *Persian art* or *the Persian style*, which admits no transformational derivation from an analogue of (51iii). As to case (iv), consider the phrase *an American attempt to attack Cuba has been expected for many years*. It is difficult to see how this could arise from a source analogous to that postulated for (50iv) (worse still, consider: *lots of American attempts to attack Cuba have failed*). In the case of (50i), there are, as Postal notes, several meanings. Thus consider (52):

(52)   (i) American offers to join a cane-cutting brigade
       (ii) Anglo-American difficulties over trade
       (iii) the Anglo-American commission
       (iv) The Anglo-American refusal to aid Biafra
       (v) the Caribbean alliance

In the case of (52i) the meaning is *offers by Americans*, not

---

argument for a lexicalist approach is far stronger in the case of derived nominals because of the clustering of properties noted earlier.

[37] Given, that is, his assumption that meaning is determined by the initial phrase-marker of a derivation. Notice that the distinction in meaning suffices to undermine Postal's inference from sharing of formal properties (selectional relations, etc.) to identity of source. At best, this line of argument is extremely weak (see Chomsky, 1968b, for some discussion), and as these examples show, is untenable in the present instance.

America's offers.[38] In (52ii) the meaning is *difficulties arising between England and America.* In (52iii) the meaning is *commission formed by England and America (or constituted of representatives chosen...).* The phrase (52iv) means something like *the agreement by England and America that each refuse to aid Biafra* (i.e., their joint refusal individually to aid Biafra). In the case of (52v), there is no source at all. Not only do these phrases differ among themselves, but it is hard to see how any might have a reasonable underlying source from a possessive NP.

I think one must conclude, then, that at best the argument for derivation of PPA's from possessive NP's is shaky, and at worst, the facts show that there is no such derivation. This observation is of some interest, because Postal regards the conclusion that PPA's derive from NP's as "crucial for the subject of this paper". The reason is that this derivation gives the only strong argument[39] for the conclusion that transformations create "anaphoric islands", that is, phrases no part of which can appear in a relation of coreference (putting it loosely). It is clear that lexical items are such anaphoric islands. Thus to use Postal's example, we cannot say (53), meaning that Max misses his parents:

(53)   Max is an orphan and he deeply misses them

As Postal observes, this fact might serve as a prima facie argument against generative semantics, which would hold that *orphan* replaces some such structure as "person whose parents were dead". One might ask, on these grounds, why pronominalization cannot have applied prior to the transformation which inserts the word *orphan.* To show that this fact does not count against generative

---

[38]   Postal discusses such cases, arguing that they show that "generic" NP's such as *Americans* or *machine-guns* "involve the names of sets", so that PPA's are derived from the "natural class" of proper nouns and generic NP's. However, it is unclear how the name of a set is involved in (52i), or in *Americans offered to go to Cuba,* or even in the example that Postal gives to illustrate the point (namely, *machine-guns are so-called because they fire automatically —* here, as in *machine-guns misfired* the phrase *machine-guns* is not used to name a set).

[39]   Others are suggested, but as Postal would surely agree, they do not carry much weight.

semantics, it is crucial, Postal argues, to demonstrate that there are transformations that introduce anaphoric islands. Then the fact that lexical insertion operations introduce anaphoric islands will not require a unique condition designed ad hoc to solve a problem that arises within the framework of generative semantics. Hence the importance of demonstrating that the PPA's (which, as Postal shows, are anaphoric islands) are introduced transformationally. Correspondingly, when the latter argument collapses, as I think it does, we are left with an argument (insignificant, in my opinion) against generative semantics: namely, it requires that lexical insertion operations have the ad hoc property, not motivated by any other consideration, that they create anaphoric islands. Obviously, this is a problem that does not arise in the (extended) standard theory.

The correct generalization seems to be that items that have a lexical entry are "anaphoric islands". Thus nouns, verbs, adjectives, and idioms are anaphoric islands. There are no anaphoric processes "internal" to such expressions as *orphan, book, American, lighthouse keeper, kick the bucket,*[40] etc. No doubt refinements are needed, but this seems to be the basic principle. It is expressible easily in terms of the notion "lexical entry". Again, these considerations seem to me to add some slight support for a theory such as the (extended) standard theory that incorporates this notion in an essential way.

---

[40] That is, one cannot say *John kicked the bucket and Bill kicked it too,* meaning both died. It should be noted, incidentally, that idioms would appear to be a difficult problem for generative semantics in the first place. An interpretive system can simply provide interpretive rules for certain well-formed phrases, but the generative semantics approach will leave unexplained the fact that, characteristically idioms have normal grammatical structure; e.g., if *kick the bucket* is introduced by transformation from an underlying phrase-marker *die* or *become not alive*, why does it have the internal structure of a normal verb phrase? The problem is analogous to several that we have discussed earlier.

Notice, incidentally, that however *lighthouse keeper* enters a derivation, it must be assigned its meaning by an ad hoc rule, since it is not synonymous with *person who keeps a lighthouse* — i.e., *keep* in this idiom does not, strictly speaking, have exactly the same meaning as in *John kept the gift, keep house,* etc.

6.7. I have tried to show, in 6, that there is no evidence against the narrower and more restrictive (hence preferable) assumptions of the (extended) standard theory with regard to lexical insertion. On the contrary, it seems that there are good reasons to suppose that all lexical insertion rules precede any nonlexical transformation, so that the notion "deep structure" is defined and conditions on deep structure can be formulated to constrain derivations. These conditions are the rules of the base, including the lexical insertion rules (which appear to meet the constraints on contextual features outlined in Chomsky, 1965) and the categorial rules that define the initial phrase-marker P_1 of a derivation Σ. The latter rules, in turn, can in part be generalized as schemata of the sort discussed in Chomsky (1967), so it seems. In these terms, we can account for striking regularities in form and convergence of properties that are expressible at the level of deep structure, though apparently not elsewhere.

6.8.1. The earliest work in generative grammar noted explicitly that the grammatical relations expressed in deep structure (as we are now calling it) do not correspond, one-to-one, to significant semantic properties, and the observation is, of course, familiar from traditional grammar. Within the framework of the standard theory or the proposed extension, rules must be formulated determining the semantic relations that hold of items in the deep structure, on the basis of the grammatical relations of the deep structure and specific properties of the lexical items themselves. To take a concrete example, consider the word *break* as it appears in the sentences of (54):[41]

(54)   (i) the window broke
        (ii) a hammer broke the window
        (iii) the workman broke the window with a hammer
        (iv) the window broke with a hammer

[41] The examples are from Matthews (1968). He notes that such sentences as (54iv), though perhaps dubious in isolation, are motivated by other examples, such as *the window won't break, even with a hammer, the window broke easily with a hammer*, etc.

   (v) the child's toy broke against the tree trunk
  (vi) the bully broke the child's toy against the tree trunk
 (vii) the news broke (to the public)
(viii) a doctor broke the news (to the public) (with a
      telegram)
  (ix) a telegram broke the news

Following Matthews' terminology, let us specify the semantic relations by assigning "cases" to the noun phrases as follows: animate agent is nominative; thing or person acted upon or toward is dative; thing used is instrumental; thing acted upon but not modified by the action is absolutive; place where is locative. Then in the examples (54), *window* is dative; *hammer* is instrumental; *workman* is nominative; *toy* is dative; *tree trunk* is locative; *bully* is nominative; *news* is absolutive; *public* is dative; *doctor* is nominative; *telegram* is instrumental. Suppose that the deep structures are similar to the surface structures in (54). Then the cases do not directly reflect deep structure grammatical relations. For example, *the window* is subject in (i) and object in (ii), but is dative in both cases; the subject is dative in (i) and instrumental in (ii); etc. Even on this assumption, we might, however, determine the cases by simple rules that use the grammatical relations of the deep structure and certain lexical properties of *break*. Suppose that *break* is entered in the lexicon with this specification:

(55)   *break* is intransitive or causative; it optionally takes locative and instrumental; the subject of the intransitive is dative or absolutive.

The terms "subject" and "intransitive" are defined in the obvious way in terms of deep structure; the term "causative" is so defined that a verb with the feature [+causative] appears in the context subject-object, where the object is the subject of the corresponding intransitive (see Chomsky, 1965, 1967). Thus the lexical entry (55) specifies that *break* can appear in the contexts of (56), in deep structure, where NP_1 can be either dative or absolutive:

(56)   (i) NP$_1$ — (loc) (instr)

$$\text{(ii) NP}_2 \begin{bmatrix} - \\ +\text{caus} \end{bmatrix} \text{NP}_1 \text{ (loc) (instr)}$$

A general rule specifies that the subject of a transitive verb of action (i.e., a verb such as *give* but not *receive*), can be an agent (nominative) if it is animate; otherwise it is instrumental. Choice of dative or absolutive is contingent on concreteness versus abstractness of the noun phrase.

With these definitions and the specification (55), cases (i.e., semantic relations) are assigned properly in (54), and other possible examples are excluded.

6.8.2. Matthews suggests a different approach to this set of facts. He proposes that the central rule of the base grammar generate the structure (57):

(57)   it — Aux — [V (NP) (NP)...]$_{\text{prop}}$

The word *break* (similarly, every verb) imposes certain cases on the NP's that follow it in the proposition (prop). Thus *break* would be entered in the lexicon with the following specification:

(58)   *break*: — (abs)$_a$(dat)$_b$(loc)(instr)(nom), where either a or b must appear.

A general transformational rule takes an NP of prop in (57) and substitutes it for the subject *it*, under the following conditions:

(59)   the rule applies to the final NP of prop when it is nominative, and optionally to the final NP of prop when it is instrumental: otherwise, it applies to the NP following the verb.

This approach, too, accounts for the phenomena of (54). Further refinements are possible in both cases, but the general ideas are clear. Both approaches are formulable within the (extended) standard theory. In fact, it might be questioned whether they are more than notational variants. Perhaps empirical differences can be determined. If not, we can think of them as alternative ways of assigning semantic functions on the basis of lexical properties and grammatical relations of the deep structure.

6.8.3. Matthews' systems is an expanded and modified version of some ideas of Fillmore (1968). Fillmore proposes a system with underlying case representations that are not phrase-markers at all. Thus he would interpret the proposition of (57) as an unordered set $(V, C_1,...,C_n)$, where the C_i's are various cases. A particular verb can be associated with V when its lexical entry and the cases of prop correspond; appropriate noun phrases can be associated with the C_i's. The grammar then contains two categories of rule. Rules of category I map case systems into phrase-markers.[42] For example, he would formulate a rule analogous to Matthews' (59) as a category I rule. The rules of category II are transformations which generate derivations in the usual way.

As Fillmore actually presents his system, it differs greatly from earlier versions of syntax. The basic differences, however, do not appear to be at the conceptual or theoretical level, but rather at the level of application to the particular grammar of English. Thus Fillmore takes the passive rule to be not a transformation of category II, but rather a rule of category I. It would be quite consistent with his theory of case grammar to regard passive as a transformation, rather than a rule mapping case structure onto phrase-markers. There are clear empirical differences between these two proposals concerning the status of passive. I think that Fillmore's proposal is incorrect,[43] but this is a matter of choice of grammar, not choice of linguistic theory.

[42] It appears that he construes this as a one-step mapping, not decomposable into iterated rules of category I.

[43] For several arguments, see Dougherty (forthcoming). In particular, Dougherty shows that Fillmore's rules of preposition-insertion, when properly extended, require a condition that amounts to an independent reformulation of the passive transformation, and he discusses other difficulties as well. Ross has noted other problems (personal communication). Thus the assignment of the correct passives to such sentences as *John argued with Bill about money (about money with Bill)* leads to considerable complexity, on Fillmore's assumption.

Fillmore argues that there are significant conceptual differences between case grammar and the standard theory. Specifically, he holds that:

...it is likely that... syntactic deep structure [independently motivated on syntactic grounds]... is going to go the way of the phoneme. It is an artificial intermediate level between the empirically discoverable 'semantic deep structure' [i.e., the case system] and the observationally accessible surface structure, a level the properties of which have more to do with the methodological commitments of grammarians than with the nature of human language.

This conclusion has something of the flavor of generative semantics, in the sense discussed earlier. It is quite different from our tentative conclusion, a moment ago, that case grammar may not be empirically distinguishable from the standard theory, but may merely offer another notation for expressing the relation between deep structures and semantic relations.

Fillmore's assumption relies heavily on the hypothesis that the case systems express the meaning of the sentence, or in other words, that the rules of category I are meaning-preserving. He observes, however, that this hypothesis is not true in general. Consider his examples (60), (61):

(60)   bees are swarming in the garden
(61)   the garden is swarming with bees.

Clearly these are not synonymous. It might be that *bees are swarming in the garden* [i.e., around their nest] *but most of the garden has no bees in it*, but replacement of (60) by (61) in the italicized expression yields a contradiction. Yet (60) and (61) derive from the same case representation. Fillmore suggests that this is a matter of a "focussing difference" with some "cognitive content". The problem, however, seems to me more serious than this remark would suggest. Other examples, similar to Fillmore's, are noted by Dougherty (forthcoming). I suspect that only rarely is there true synonymy among the various sentences that are derived by different rules of category I from a single case representation, and that the example (60), (61) is rather typical, not exceptional.

Fillmore's reference to a "focussing difference" suggests that the difficulty might be overcome, within his system, by adding rules of surface structure interpretation that determine focus. Unfortunately, this is impossible. The distinction is not a property of surface structure, as we can see from such examples as (62):

(62)   (i) bees are certain to be swarming in the garden
       (ii) bees were believed to be swarming in the garden
      (iii) it is in the garden that bees are swarming
       (iv) it is bees that are swarming in the garden

These differ from one another and from (60) in surface structure, but all share the relevant semantic property; similarly, the different semantic property of (61) is shared by sentences with a variety of surface structures. The relevant distinction is stateable only at a more abstract level of derivation, in fact, at the level of deep structure in the sense of the (extended) standard theory. In Fillmore's terms, it is the structure formed by the rules of category I, prior to any syntactic transformation of category II, that determines the relevant semantic properties. The same is true in many other cases. Therefore, it seems to me that Fillmore's examples contradict his conclusion quoted above; they indicate, rather, that deep structure plays a significant role in determining semantic interpretation.

An even more critical example is provided in Fillmore's discussion of what he takes to be the explanatory power of case grammar. He argues that this theory makes it possible to capture the generalization (63):

(63)   "the subject of an active transitive sentence must be interpretable as a personal agent just in case the sentence contains a *with* phrase of instrumental import."

The sentence (54iii) is an example, and such a sentence as "*a hammer broke the window with a chisel*" can only be interpreted as personification metaphor (note that (54vi) violates (63), however, since (63) asserts that containing a *with* phrase is a necessary condition for obligatory interpretation of the subject as personal agent). Fillmore notes that the sentence (64) appears to constitute an exception to (63):

(64)   the car broke the window with its fender

In this case *car* is certainly not a personal agent; rather, it appears to be instrumental, in his terms. But, he argues, both (64) and (65) derive from the case representation (66), with *the window* specified as objective and *the car's fender* as instrumental:

(65)   the car's fender broke the window
(66)   [V, *break*], [obj, *the window*], [instr, *the car's-fender*]

He suggests that the rules of category I that choose the subject "allow an option in this case: either the entire instrument phrase may appear as the subject (as in (65)), or the 'possessor' alone may be made the subject, the remainder of the instrument phrase appearing with the preposition *with* (as in (64))" (numbering changed). He then concludes:

The superficial nature of the notion 'subject of a sentence' is made apparent by these examples in a particularly persuasive way, because in the possessor-as-subject cases, the 'subject' is not even a major constituent of the sentence; it is taken from the modifier of one of the major constituents.[44]

It seems to me, however, that such examples do in fact show the inadequacy of (63). Much more important, these examples, contrary to the quoted conclusion, demonstrate the significance of the grammatical relations of deep structure. The phrase *the car* in (64) (but not (65)) seems to function as a kind of an agent. Suppose, for

[44] As further support, Fillmore claims that when the possessor is extracted by the subject-choosing rule, the possessive pronoun *its* must be left as a residue. Thus we cannot say *the car broke the window with a fender*. I doubt the accuracy of this observation; we can surely say *the car hit the window with both fenders*. In any event, the force of the observation is unclear, even to the extent that it may be accurate. Thus if something like (65) is taken as deep structure, the choice of *its* will be determined by general rules that are independently needed, as in *John lost his way, John hit the window with his head*, etc. See note 45.

example, that the laws of nature were changed in such a way that when a car is produced there is also, necessarily, a paired anti-car produced along with it, called its *twin*, the two then being independent of one another. Then from (67) we should, by Fillmore's rules, be able to form the synonymous pair (68):

(67)   [V, *break*], [obj, *the window*], [instr, *the car's-twin*]
(68)   (i) the car broke the window with its twin (parallel to (64))
        (ii) the car's twin broke the window (parallel to (65)).

Of course, these are not synonymous. The reason is that in some sense the car is performing the action in (64) and (68i), but not in (65) and (68ii). In other words, exactly as in the case of (60)-(61), the grammatical relations expressed in the phrase-marker formed by the category I rules play a role in determining the meaning of the sentence.

We might seek to remedy this defect by restricting the operation of the category I rule of subject-choosing to only certain kinds of possession, say to possession of a part. To see the technical difficulties to which this suggestion would give rise, consider the case of two cars with radio antennas, one of the normal sort, one with an independent motor that raises and lowers the antenna. Consider the sentences (70) derived from the case structure (69):

(69)   [V, *hit*], [obj, *the garage roof*], [instr, *my car's-radio antenna*]
(70)   (i) my car hit the garage roof with its radio antenna
        (ii) my car's radio antenna hit the garage roof

Sentence (70ii) has approximately the sense of (70i) in the case of the car with the normal antenna; but if the motor of the antenna independently caused the antenna to rise, hitting the garage roof while the car was parked in the garage, we could truly say (70ii) but not (70i). The reason, again, is that some sort of "agency" is associated with the subject position in (70).

Still a further difficulty is noted by Dougherty (forthcoming). Consider the sentences (71):

(71)   (i) Caruso broke the window with his voice
       (ii) Caruso's voice broke the window

These derive from (72), but (71i) also derives, independently, from (73):

(72)   [V, *break*], [obj, *the window*], [instr, *Caruso's-voice*]
(73)   [V, *break*], [obj, *the window*], [instr, *voice*], [agent, *Caruso*]

However, there is no ambiguity in (71i).[45] Thus an unambiguous structure derives from two distinct case representations. This can be reconciled with the assumption that case representation relates directly to meaning only if we accept the conclusion that the cases are not an independent set of semantic primitives, a conclusion that appears inconsistent with Fillmore's general assumptions. On the other hand, the observations noted are just what would follow from the assumption that the grammatical relations of the deep structure, taken together with the lexical properties of particular verbs, determine the semantically significant grammatical relations.

I think that these considerations show, fairly persuasively, that the very examples that Fillmore discusses to illustrate the explanatory power of case grammar and the "superficial" character of deep structure grammatical relations, in fact demonstrate the opposite. The grammatical relations of the deep structure appear to play a central role in determining the meaning. The case representation appears to be nothing more than a notation to express what the standard theory would express in the form (55).[46]

Other examples that Fillmore discusses seem to me to lead to the same conclusion. To mention just one, consider the sentences (74):

---

[45] Furthermore, the derivation of (71i) from (73) shows that *his* must be introduced quite apart from the rule of selection of possessor of the instrument phrase.

[46] Fillmore cites only one other example of the "explanatory force" of case grammar, namely, in connection with certain restrictions on conjunction. Dougherty (forthcoming) shows that at the very least, more cases will be needed to account for the restrictions on conjunction. I suspect that the restrictions on conjunction do not involve cases at all; rather, there is a gradation of acceptability of conjunction depending on a variety of properties of conjoined elements.

(74)   (i) Mary pinched John on the nose

        (ii) Mary pinched John's nose

Fillmore would derive these from (75), by a category I rule analogous to the rule of subject-choosing just discussed:

(75)   [V, *pinch*], [loc, *John's-nose*], [agent, *Mary*][47]

According to his analysis, either *John* or *John's nose* can be "promoted" to a major constituent by the category I rules, just as either *the car* or *the car's fender* could be promoted in (64)-(66).

Here too, however, the analysis seems to me defective. Thus suppose that *pinch* is replaced by *pull* in (75). Then we can have the analogue to (74ii), but not (74i).[48] Surely the difference is related to the fact that the sentences of (76) are well-formed, but not those that result from replacement of *pinch* by *pull* in (76):

(76)   Mary pinched John near the nose, behind his left ear, etc.

In short, *pinch*, but not *pull*, appears freely in the frame: — NP PP. The sentence (74i), then, is just one special case of this general deep structure pattern, while (74ii) is an instance of the pattern: — NP. The fact that *nose* bears a part-whole relation to *John* in (74i) is a general property of such phrases as "on the nose" (compare, e.g., the examples of note 48).

In this set of examples too it is the deep structure patterns that are crucial for determining form and meaning. The case representations are best understood as a notation for expressing the semantic relations determined by the interplay of deep structure grammatical relations and specific properties of particular lexical items. It seems to me that all of these considerations support the standard theory (or the proposed extension), rather than the conclusions that Fillmore draws.

---

[47]   Actually, a further analysis is suggested for *John's nose*, but this is irrelevant here.

[48]   There is, of course, the sentence *Mary pulled John by the nose*, but this surely must have a very different source, if meaning is to be expressed correctly. Similarly, compare *Mary pulled John's hair*, *Mary pulled John by the hair*, * *Mary pulled John on the hair*, etc.

6.8.4. Summarizing this discussion, it seems to me that presently available evidence leads us to accept the hypotheses of the revised standard theory concerning lexical insertion, deep structure, and grammatical relations.[49]

7.0. Let us turn now to a different matter. As noted earlier, the extended standard theory permits only base rules, transformational rules, a simple output condition on surface structures (and certain other conditions — see note 12), and rules of interpretation applying to deep and surface (perhaps also shallow) structures. To be more precise, the latter rules apply to phonetically interpreted surface structures. Furthermore, there are general conditions on the application of transformations of the sort discussed in § 2.1. As already noted, recent work in generative semantics has suggested that there may be many other types of rules (derivational constraints). It would hardly come as a surprise to discover that this is true. Nevertheless, any such enrichment of linguistic theory must, of course, be empirically well-motivated and, furthermore, we will naturally seek a narrow formulation of any richer devices, if they are empirically motivated, for reasons discussed in § 2.2. Let us consider a few concrete examples that have been proposed to illustrate the need to enrich the framework of linguistic theory by permitting new kinds of rules, and thus a much wider variety of possible grammars.

7.1.1. One concrete question that has been discussed in some detail concerns quantifiers and negation in English. Consider the sentences (77), (78):

(77)   many men read few books
(78)   few books are read by many men

Such sentences were suggested by Jackendoff (1969)[50] to illustrate the difference in meaning of paired active-passive sentences.

---

[49] For some very interesting discussion of how semantic relations can be determined from deep structure, and some possible semantic and syntactic consequences, see Jackendoff (1969), p. 74ff., developing some ideas of Gruber (1965).
[50] See also earlier work of his cited there.

Clearly the sentences do differ in meaning, and equally obviously, the difference is related to the order of the quantifiers in surface structure. Jackendoff proposed that the order and scope of quantifiers and negation is determined from the surface structure, in accordance with what I have here called the "extended standard theory".

Lakoff has suggested an alternative analysis, within the framework of generative semantics. He proposes that the underlying structures for (77) and (78) are essentially (77') and (78') respectively:

(77')   (78')

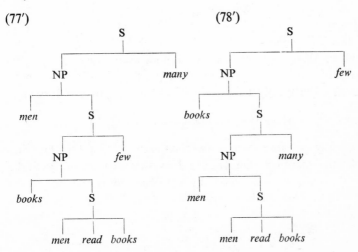

A rule of "quantifier lowering" is then formulated which, in (77'), first inserts *few* before *books* and then (on the next cycle) *many* before *men* (similarly, in (78'), with the order reversed). A new derivational constraint guarantees that the "height" of the quantifier in deep structure corresponds to left-to-right order in surface structure, in the simplest cases, to which I will restrict attention.[51] Presumably, the relative clause condition will exclude such deep structures as (79):

[51] For the purposes of comparison of theories, nothing is lost by this restriction. Comparable complications arise in the alternative theories as further complexity is introduced.

(79)

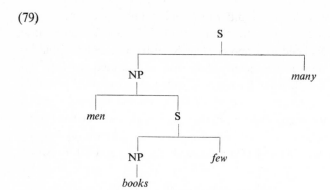

— i.e., (77′) with the most deeply embedded S missing.

Given this apparatus, we can say that deep structure (or P_1 of the derivation) relates directly to "logical form". Thus we could convert (77′) directly to a pseudo-quantificational form such as (80):

(80)   for many $x\varepsilon$ Men, for few $y\varepsilon$ Books, x read y

Exactly the same is true if we drop the rule of quantifier lowering from the grammar, eliminate the derivational constraint, and take the deep structure of (77) and (78) to be (approximately):

(81)

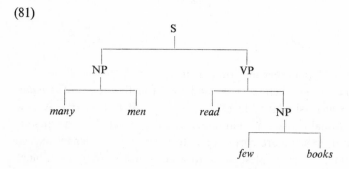

with (78) formed by the ordinary passive transformation. There is a trivial algorithm which, applied to the surface structures, gives the pseudo-quantificational forms such as (80).

Here then is a simple case where a rule of surface structure interpretation can be rephrased in terms of a derivational constraint and a new transformation. Is there any point to this? I think not, for several reasons.

Notice first that the structures in which quantifiers appear as predicates have unique properties. For example, the structure (79) is admissible only if the embedded NP *books* has a relative clause attached to it; furthermore, this relative clause must contain both of the NP's that appear in (79). These conditions are without parallel among syntactically motivated structures. Furthermore, although (77′) appears to involve a "relative clause", this structure is unique in that its antecedent, *men*, does not appear within the "relative clause" of which it is the immediate antecedent.

Furthermore, NP's which appear in non-relativizable positions can of course contain quantifiers, and will thus appear in these new pseudo-relative structures. Consider for example the sentence (82):

(82)   Che's strategy of many Vietnams will succeed.

Presumably, in accordance with this theory, the structure underlying the NP subject is something like (83), just as the structure underlying *men read many books* is (84):

(83)   [*Vietnams* [*Che's strategy of Vietnams*] *many*]
(84)   [*books* [*men read books*] *many*]

But whereas in (84) *books* is in a relativizable position (compare *the books that men read are...*), in (83) *Vietnams* is not in a relativizable position (compare *Vietnams, Che's strategy of which, are...*). Yet both (83) and (84), or something like them, must be presupposed, and the rules of relativization (e.g., *wh*-movement) must apply in both, although general conditions on transformations (cf. § 2.1., above) preclude this in the case of (83). Further problems arise when we ask how (83) fits into the rest of the sentence, or if we consider such sentences as (85):

(85)   Several strategies of many Vietnams will fail, but one will finally succeed.

Nevertheless, the unique properties of these new relative and predicate structures can be "isolated" from the remainder of the grammar. However the constraints on relativization are ultimately to be formulated, there is little doubt that they will be formulable so as to permit these particular cases of non-relativizable relatives. The reason has to do with the operation of quantifier-lowering, which was formulated *ad hoc* for this case, and is itself quite unlike any syntactically motivated transformation in its properties. (Note that this is a further argument against, not a consideration in favor of this theory.)

The rule of quantifier-lowering deletes the antecedent noun and moves the predicate of the matrix sentence into the embedded sentence. Thus applying to (84), it deletes *books* in the matrix structure and inserts *many* into the embedded "relative".[52] Neither of these operations has an analogue within the syntactically motivated sections of the grammar. In particular, although there are a number of rules which extract items from an embedded sentence and move them into higher sentences, there is, to my knowledge, none that introduces an item into a phrase of an embedded sentence from outside of this sentence. In fact, it has been proposed (cf. Chomsky, 1965) that there is a universal condition blocking such rules.[53] This was suggested as a possible way of

---

[52]   The only function of the antecedent is to identify the noun to which the quantifier is attached. Thus we could just as well eliminate the antecedents *men* and *books* in (77′), (78′), (79) and assign appropriate indices to the two predicates *many* and *few*, and the words *men* and *books*, in the most deeply embedded sentence. Then the rule of quantifier-lowering can be simplified, since it need not delete the antecedent. Taking the argument one step further, we can eliminate the rule and the indices entirely by assigning the quantifier to the noun phrases with which it shares an index. With these relatively slight modifications we return to a deep structure of a familiar sort, rather like the surface structure. As already noted, it can be related directly to the pseudo-quantificational form (80). Lakoff notes that in some cases the quantifier appears in the predicate (*the men who read books were many*, though of course in some cases it cannot (**the men who read the book were a lot, *the enthusiasm that he showed me was little*). I see no way to construct an argument, one way or another, on the basis of these observations. It is worth noting that when the quantifier appears in predicate position, its semantic relation to the subject is entirely different from any other subject-predicate relation.

[53]   To formulate such a condition precisely and completely is no easier than in the case of the other general conditions on transformations, most of which have unexplained inadequacies. But, as in the other cases, the general lines of a formulation can be stated, subject to further sharpening.

explaining the familiar observation that reflexivization and "inherent coreference" (see Helke, 1969) is impermissible in the case of embedded sentences, as in * *John expected Mary to hurt himself,* * *John expected Mary to lose his mind.* Dougherty (1968) observes that under an analysis that he develops in detail, the same general condition would explain the fact that from (86) we can form (87), but from (88) we cannot form (89):

(86)   each of the men saw the others
(87)   (i) the men each saw the others
         (ii) the men saw each other
(88)   each of the men expected the police to catch the others
(89)   the men expected the police to catch each other

Moreover, the rule of quantifier-lowering appears to violate the constraints suggested by Emonds (1969) for cyclic rules.

Thus the proposal under investigation sets up structures with unique properties and requires rules that violate otherwise plausible conditions on the application of rules. None of these arguments against this proposal is decisive — there is no such thing as a completely decisive argument in the present state of the field — but they do suggest that the proposal is incorrect, and specifically, that quantifier-lowering is not only a syntactically unmotivated rule of a unique character, but also perhaps an impossible rule, on general grounds.

These considerations, then, seem to me to support an approach rather like that of Jackendoff (1969), in which the syntax is left in the simplest possible form, there is no rule of quantifier-lowering, no unique structures and rules, and no new sorts of derivational constraints. Rather, a rule of interpretation determines "logical form" from surface structure (just as in the alternative theory, a rule of interpretation might map (77′) into (80), in some more "canonical" notation – see note 52). This rule of interpretation, incidentally, need be formulated as part of a grammar only to the extent that it is language-specific.

7.1.2. Before we leave this topic, several other observations are in order. Lakoff notes that it is not just surface structure, but some structure prior to deletion operations that relates to "logical form". Consider, for example, the sentence (90):

(90)   Jane isn't liked by many men, and Sally isn't either

We must know, in interpreting this sentence, how *many* functions with respect to the second conjunct. This observation is correct, and would require a modification of Jackendoff's theory of semantic interpretation to permit also consideration of shallow structure (in the sense of note 6) if in fact there is a deletion operation involved in such sentences as (90). There are arguments for the latter hypothesis, but there are arguments against it as well. Consider, for example, the sentences (91)-(93):

(91)   John hasn't been here for a month
(92)   John has been here for a month
(93)   John hasn't been here for a month, but Bill has

The sentence (91) is ambiguous: it may be used to deny (92), meaning that John hasn't spent the entire month here; or, more naturally, it may be interpreted as meaning that there is no time during the past month when John was here, i.e., he hasn't been here even once. (This seems to me, furthermore, the only interpretation when *hasn't* is unstressed.) But sentence (92) is unambiguous, having only the interpretation: for all of the time during the last month, John has been here — i.e., he didn't just appear now and then, but spent the month here.[54] Sentence (92) cannot have the meaning *John has been here at some time during the month*, i.e., the proposition denied under the second interpretation of (91). But now consider (93). Where the first conjunct is interpreted (in the natural way) to mean *it is not the case that John has been here at some time during the month* (i.e., *there is no time during the month when John was here*), the second conjunct means *Bill has been here at some time during the month*. Thus if (94) underlies (93),

---

[54] I overlook, as irrelevant to this distinction, a more precise statement of what it means to be here for a month.

then the second conjunct in (94) has an interpretation which it cannot have in isolation:

(94)   John hasn't been here for a month, but Bill has been here for a month.

There are many similar examples, some of which even have syntactic residues; consider, for example, (95)-(96):

(95)   John won't leave until midnight, but Bill will
(96)   * Bill will leave until midnight.

In the case of (95)-(96) one might propose an "output condition" that excludes (96) in isolation while permitting it as an underlying conjunct of (95). To extend such a solution to (91)-(93), one would have to say that (92) too is ambiguous, but that some sort of "output condition" eliminates one interpretation when it appears in isolation. Perhaps such a proposal can be given a coherent formulation. But such an enrichment of the theory of grammar seems to me a rather questionable move. More natural, I think, is the conclusion that (93) and (96) are not formed by deletion operations, and that "compositional semantics" must be abandoned (or at least restricted), with the semantic interpretation in such cases as (93) constructed along lines that have been explored by Jackendoff (1969) and Akmajian (1969).

There are other examples that suggest that rather complex aspects of semantic representation must be constructed from surface structure. Consider the sentence (97):

(97)   it is being regarded as incompetent that disturbs John

There are general principles determining focus and presupposition from surface structure which, applied to (97), specify the focus as (98) and the presupposition as (99):

(98)   being regarded as incompetent
(99)   something disturbs John

See Chomsky (1968b). (The point is perhaps still clearer when (97) is negated.) These conclusions seem correct, but of course the property expressed by (98) is not associated with a deep structure phrase. The predicate *regard X as incompetent* expressed by (98) poses no problems of principle, but it is a predicate that is expressed only by a phrase of surface structure. The question that remains important, and essentially unanswered in any interesting way, is how such predicates are constructed and interpreted, given the full derivation Σ. Such considerations suggest that surface structure may contribute new predicates, as well as certain aspects of "logical form".

The problems posed by (90), and the general question of whether "shallow structure" must be considered along with surface structure in the revised theory, must, I think, be held in abeyance until these more general issues are resolved.

7.1.3. I think that a somewhat more careful look at the semantics of quantifiers and negation lends further support to an interpretive theory of the sort that Jackendoff has suggested. The examples (77) and (78) involved the quantifier *few*, which is inherently negative, meaning "not many". This is crucial. If, in these examples, *few* is replaced, say, by *a few* or *several*, it is much less clear that there is a difference of meaning between the modified (77) and (78), or that left-to-right order in surface structure corresponds, in such a simple way, to order of quantifiers in a canonical notation such as (80). Looking at the matter more closely, consider Jackendoff's sentences (100), (101):

(100)   not many arrows hit the target
(101)   the target was not hit by many arrows.

Jackendoff and Lakoff have argued that these sentences are synonymous on one reading (they disagree as to whether the second is ambiguous, a matter that is irrelevant here), meaning: *it is not so that many arrows hit the target*. Others have also accepted this conclusion (e.g., Chomsky, 1968b). However, I do not think that it is strictly true. There is a clear difference in presupposition. Sentence (100) (equivalently, *few arrows hit the target)* presupposes that some arrows hit the target, but sentence (101) does not; (101), but not (100), is properly paraphrased as *it is not so that many arrows hit the target*. Imagine a situation in which no arrows hit the target and someone asserts that many arrows hit the target. We could deny his assertion by saying *it is not so that many arrows hit the target*, or *the target was not hit by many arrows* (= (101), this interpretation perhaps requires stress on *not*), but we would not deny it, in this case, by saying: *you're wrong, not many (few) arrows hit the target*. Such a response is inappropriate because of the expressed presupposition that at least some arrows hit the target.

There is a similar distinction in the analogous case of non-count nouns and their quantifiers. The sentence *little enthusiasm was shown for that project* (equivalently, *not much enthusiasm was shown for that project*) cannot be paraphrased as *it is not so that much enthusiasm was shown for that project* because it presupposes, as the proposed paraphrase does not, that at least some enthusiasm was shown. Thus if we know that no enthusiasm was shown we would not deny the assertion that much enthusiasm was shown by saying: *not much enthusiasm was shown for the project*.

Discussion of presupposition is made difficult by the fact that there are a number of different kinds of presupposition that have not been distinguished with sufficient clarity. Thus consider the sentence (102):

(102)   two of my five children are in elementary school.

The statement of (102) presupposes that I have five children; if I have six children, the statement is without truth value. In quite another sense, (102) presupposes that three of my five children are not in elementary school. That is, it would be natural for the hearer to assume this, on the basis of the statement (102). On the other hand, if, in fact, three are in elementary school, (102) is not devoid of truth value; in fact it is true. Hearing (102), one is entitled to assume that three of my children are not in elementary school, perhaps by virtue of general conditions on discourse of a sort that have been discussed by Paul Grice in his work on "conversational implicature". However, it is easy to imagine conditions under which this assumption would be withdrawn and it would be perfectly appropriate to say *two of my five children are in elementary school, and so are the other three;* but there are no circumstances under which the presupposition of (102) that I have exactly five children can be withdrawn.

The presupposition of (100) that some arrows hit the target seems to me of the latter sort. One might argue that insofar as presuppositions can be explained in terms of general "maxims of discourse" (in the Gricean sense) they need not be made explicit in the grammar of a particular language.[55] But the presuppositions associated with *few arrows* (or *not many arrows,* or *little enthusiasm,* or *not much enthusiasm)* or with *five children* in (102) do not appear to me to be of this sort, and it seems natural to require that a theory of grammar incorporate them. It would be of some interest to develop sharper analytic criteria in this area.

The matter is important, in the present connection, because of its bearing on the problem of "constituent negation", a central notion in Jackendoff's theory. In the sentence (100), the negative element is associated in surface structure with the first noun phrase. Similarly, in (103) it is associated with a noun phrase:

(103)   John and Bill are arguing about nothing.

In the sentence (104), we can take the negative element to be associated with the verb, so that it means *John dislikes mushrooms,* or with the verb phrase, in which case it means: *it is not so that John likes mushrooms:*

(104)   John [(doesn't like) mushrooms].

In other words, either the parentheses or the brackets express a possible interpretation. Perhaps the same ambiguous interpretation is possible in the case of (101). It appears that interpretation as "sentence negation" without a specific presupposition is appropriate only when the negative element is associated with the predicate phrase. In the other cases, there seems to be a specific presupposi-

---

[55]   Observe that there are two questions intermingled here, one having to do with the universality of the maxims, the second, with the question whether they belong to "grammar" or to some other study, perhaps a theory of performance.

tion, as we have noted in the case of (100). Thus (103) presupposes that John and Bill are arguing, and asserts that there is no substance to their disagreement.[56] In (104), if we associate the negative element with the verb *like*, so that the meaning is *John dislikes mushrooms*, there is a presupposition that he has the relevant experience with mushrooms, but this is not the case when negation is associated with the entire predicate phrase. Thus if John has never tasted mushrooms and it is asserted that he likes them, I can deny the assertion by stating (104), interpreting the negation as associated with the predicate phrase, but not by stating *John dislikes mushrooms*, or (104) with the negation interpreted as associated with the verb.[57]

Though much remains unclear, it does seem that the actual position of the negative element in surface structure is quite critical, and that when it is not associated with the verb phrase, there are specific presuppositions that are otherwise lacking. These observations suggest that the position of the negative element plays a role in determining what is presupposed as well as what is asserted, and that "canonical paraphrase" in which negation is treated simply as associated with propositions, though perhaps possible with some artificiality, may well be an irrelevant sidetrack.[58]

---

[56] Note that *nothing* must receive main stress in (103), as distinct from *something* in *John and Bill are arguing about something*, which is normally unstressed. Some connections between position of main stress and presupposition (in one sense) are discussed in Chomsky (1968b).

[57] Again, the matter of stress placement is critical. Consider, in the same connection, the presupposition and assertion of the negation of (97).

[58] Lakoff and Ross (1969) argue that a paraphrase with sentence negation always exists, and conclude that constituent negation is therefore an unnecessary notion. The argument has no force. By the same logic, we could show that sentence negation is an unnecessary notion, since there is always a paraphrase in terms of constituent negation (i.e., *not*-S can always be paraphrased as *it is false that S* or *it is not the case that S*, where we interpret not *the case* (= *false*), as "constituent negation" (noting that "it is not the case that S" can be denied by "it is *not* not the case that S". Neither argument proves anything. The interesting question has to do with the rules and principles that determine the interpretation of the syntactic forms, and the possibilities of paraphrase in one or another canonical notation tell us virtually nothing about this.

7.2. Summarizing, a consideration of the properties of quantifiers and negations seems to support the view that syntactically motivated rules and the structures they involve suffice to account for whatever facts are clear, in a fairly natural way, and that the introduction of more abstract underlying structures and transformations with no syntactic motivation (such as quantifier-lowering) simply leads to new problems and complexity, while requiring that linguistic theory be enriched to incorporate a broader class of rules (derivational constraints).

To my knowledge, this case is typical, and it supports the working hypothesis expressed in EST. If we consider simply the problem of constructing grammars that generate surface structures with the devices of the standard theory (base rules and transformations), restricting ourselves to rules that are motivated in the sense that they permit the fullest expression of significant generalizations, we are led to the construction of deep structures that do not, in their formal configurations, express directly all of the semantic properties of sentences. I know of no clear cases, however, where these properties cannot be expressed by fairly general and natural rules applying to the motivated deep and surface (and perhaps shallow) structures. Of course, there are so many unclear cases (on any grounds) that one can only be extremely hesitant about putting forward a general hypothesis. Furthermore, there are serious conceptual questions that can be raised, for example, regarding the question what are "significant generalizations". In the cases so far discussed, however, and others to which I will turn directly, postulation of more abstract structures to express semantic content and rules designed ad hoc to incorporate these more abstract structures in derivations offers at best a notational alternative, and at worst, leads to new complications. It is for this reason that I believe that the extended standard theory should, tentatively, be adopted as the framework for grammatical research.

7.3. Let me consider another case which illustrates fairly clearly what I believe to be the typical situation in this regard. Consider English modals, in particular, the modal *may*. It is well known that there is an ambiguity in such sentences as (105):

(105) John may leave tomorrow

which may be interpreted as meaning that it is permitted that John leave or that it is possible that he will leave. Lyle Jenkins, in unpublished work, has pointed out that there is a somewhat different range of interpretation that appears in interrogatives. Compare (106) and (107):

(106) may John leave the room
(107) may I (please) have the ashtray

To (106), the natural response is *Yes, he may*, or *No, he may not*. To (107), the appropriate response is something like *here, take it*, or simply the action of giving the ashtray. A mere affirmative response would be inappropriate. Sentence (106) is a question as to whether something is permitted (i.e., *may* is used in the permission sense), whereas (107) is a request for the ashtray.

Furthermore, this interpretation of a questioned *may* as a request for action depends in part on the surface subject. Thus consider the sentences (108)-(111):

(108) may I please examine you, Dr. X
(109) May I please be examined by you, Dr. X
(110) may you please examine me, Dr. X
(111) may you please be examined by me, Dr. X

Sentences (108), (109) are requests, in the sense of (107), but (110), (111) are not so interpretable, if they are well-formed at all.[59] The sentences (108), (109), do not involve either the permission sense of *may* or the possibility sense. The interpretation as a request for action is impossible in cases (110), (111), exactly as it would be if *I* were replaced by *you* in (107). It is the item that appears as surface subject of the sentence that determines whether this interpretation is possible in the case of (108)-(111).

[59] I leave open the question whether they are syntactically ill-formed, or syntactically well-formed but ruled out by the filtering function of semantic interpretive rules.

Thus in declaratives, *may* has the sense of possibility or permission, whereas in interrogatives, it may have the sense of permission or a kind of request. The interpretation, in interrogatives, depends in part on the person of the surface subject. In this case, the semantic properties seem relatively straightforward, and should be formulable in a simple way. The underlying structures are characterized in terms of simple base rules, and the transformations involved are also quite simple and straightforward. But the interpretation depends on a property of the surface structure, as is quite generally the case with modals. There is absolutely no point in introducing further transformational apparatus, or phrase-markers unmotivated by independent considerations, into the description of these phenomena. There is no need for new derivational constraints (i.e., rules) to determine the sequences of phrase-markers that constitute derivations. We can use the term "derivational constraint" to refer to the rules that relate the surface structure to the semantic representation, but this is merely a terminological point — and a misleading one, if it serves as an avenue for the introduction of much richer descriptive devices into linguistic theory.

For many other examples of this sort, see Culicover (1970).

7.4. Are there "derivational constraints" other than the rules that relate surface (or shallow) structure to semantic representation? For example, are there examples of transformational rules that cannot be formulated as mappings of phrase-markers into phrase-markers, but require rather some reference to earlier stages of derivation? Several such cases have been suggested, some in print. Generally, the "earlier stage of derivation" is the deep structure or semantic representation; a case in point was noted in the references of footnote 5, where a general condition on transformations appears to be involved.

It is clear that only certain types of examples of this sort are relevant to the (extended) standard theory. Suppose, for example, that the transformation T maps P into P' just in case P meets both the syntactic condition C on phrase-markers and the semantic condition C'. We may ask whether the following reformulation is empirically equivalent: T applies freely to phrase-markers meeting condition C, but the resulting surface structure must be interpreted by a semantic rule that incorporates C'. This alternative will not always be available, in principle. To my knowledge, it is available in every case that has been suggested. If so, these cases fall under the narrower condition just suggested; they exemplify the filtering effect of semantic interpretive rules and have no bearing on the correctness of the standard theory.

An example is cited in Lakoff (1969c) from Labov. He claims that in certain dialects, the rule of subject-auxiliary inversion can apply only when the sentence in question describes or is a request for information; equivalently, we can say that the rule applies freely, and the result must be interpreted as such a request — it will be excluded as semantically anomalous if for some reason this interpretation is impossible. As noted earlier (see p. 194), the interpretation of interrogatives in general depends upon surface structure.

Note the analogy to the discussion of well-formedness in § 1.

7.5. This discussion does not exhaust all of the examples that have been proposed to try to show the necessity for richer devices than those permitted by the revised standard theory. In a sense, any unsolved problem, any collection of phenomena that remain unexplained, constitutes a potential example of this sort, and there are, needless to say, many such cases. However, of the arguments that seek to establish some specific positive conclusion, I know of none more compelling than those that have been reviewed here.

8.1. To summarize briefly, the standard theory has been shown to have certain defects. Two general proposals for remedying these defects have been discussed: EST and generative semantics. When unclarities are removed, it seems to me that these approaches differ in three essential ways: with respect to (A) lexical insertion, (B) derivational constraints, (C) the ordering of lexical and non-lexical transformations.

As to (A), EST keeps to the assumption of the standard theory that lexical items enter into deep structures in positions dominated by lexical categories, where each lexical item contains an intrinsic account of meaning of a sort that is little understood in detail. I have no doubt that the lexicon itself has an internal structure (for example, in the case of "semantic fields"). The semantic characterization of lexical items and the structures in which they appear can be given in terms of phrase-markers and transformations, for the uninteresting reason that virtually anything intelligible can be presented in these terms. This is of course a weakness, not a strength of this mode of expression, to be overcome, one hopes, as more insight in gained into the detailed structure of the lexicon.

In contrast, generative semantics maintains that lexical items replace phrase-markers that express their meaning. This is an attractive idea, and if it were tenable, there would be good reason to take it very seriously as one approach to the description of meaning. Unfortunately, it does not seem tenable. As noted earlier, the "phrase-markers" that are replaced in lexical insertion operations vary in form without discernible limit, and no comprehensible proposal has been put forth about such a simple matter as how a lexical item in an embedded sentence can be associated with its semantic representation (in particular, the presuppositions expressed, in the case of verbs). Therefore this thesis, for the moment, seems to be at best a notational proposal with little motivation or support.

With regard to (B), there are two kinds of constraints to be considered. As to constraints internal to derivations, EST maintains that there are none (beyond transformations and general conditions on transformations), whereas generative semantics, in the formulations considered here, suggests that further conditions are permitted (freely, at least so far as the published literature indicates). Since there seem to be no plausible cases to justify richer devices, the narrower theory is to be preferred. As to constraints relating semantic representations and derivations, EST holds that there is only one category of such "constraints": namely, certain specific aspects of surface (or shallow) structure are relevant to semantic interpretation. Generative semantics again permits richer devices. Every rule of interpretation mapping surface (or shallow) structure into some aspect of meaning can be described as a "derivational constraint" (i.e., a "rule of grammar"), but not conversely. Unless examples are presented to justify the extra wealth of theoretical devices permitted in generative semantics, the narrower theory is again to be preferred, for reasons discussed in § 2.2. There seems to me to be no such justification.

The ordering of lexical and nonlexical transformations seems to me to be probably the most interesting outstanding issue. For the moment, I see no empirical reason to reject the more restrictive, hence preferable theory that restricts the ordering to lexical followed by nonlexical, uniformly. Furthermore, there seem to be strong empirical reasons in favor of this narrower hypothesis: namely, the syntactic and semantic generalizations that are formulable in terms of deep structure, but not, apparently, otherwise.

In short, it seems to me that in the few areas of substantive difference, generative semantics has been taking the wrong course. But to a certain extent, the differences between these two approaches are hardly more than notational, hence of no serious concern.

8.2. The basic property of transformations is that they map phrase-markers into phrase-markers. Each transformation applies to a phrase-marker on the basis of the formal configurations expressed in it, and quite independently of the meanings or grammatical relations expressed by these formal configurations. Thus such sentences as *John received the book, John read the book, John expected the book to be good, John gave Bill the book*, and so on, undergo the passive transformation in exactly the same way. The transformation applies blindly to any phrase-marker of the proper form, caring nothing about meanings or grammatical relations. This situation is typical; I know of no exceptions, and no counterarguments that amount to more than terminological revision, although some intriguing proposals have been put forward and should obviously be explored.

These formal operations meet fairly restrictive conditions of the sort I have mentioned. As far as I know, the trivial output conditions of the standard theory suffice (but see note 12). Furthermore, the initial phrase-markers of syntactically motivated derivations meet the conditions of a context-free grammar which is "projected" from the basic categories N, V, A by phrase structure schemata. I see no reason to weaken the condition of the standard theory that lexical insertion procedes all such transformations; rather, the evidence supports this assumption. Thus it seems to me that deep structure is a well-defined level which meets the phrase structure conditions of the base rules, defines the proper contexts for lexical insertion, and provides the appropriate grammatical relations for inter-pretation in terms of "semantic relations" or "conceptual struc-tures".

There seems to me to be no justification for any enrichment of the theory to permit other devices for "constraining derivations", i.e., other kinds of rules. Specifically, there seem to me to be no per-suasive examples of "global derivational constraints", beyond those permitted in the extended standard theory. Many aspects of meaning (scope and order of logical elements, coreference, focus and certain types of presupposition) seem to involve surface (and perhaps shallow) structure in an essential way.

A central idea in much of structural linguistics was that the formal devices of language should be studied independently of their use. The earliest work in transformational-generative grammar took over a version of this thesis, as a working hypothesis. I think it has been a fruitful hypothesis. It seems that grammars contain a substructure of perfectly formal rules operating on phrase-markers in narrowly circumscribed ways. Not only are these rules inde-pendent of meaning or sound in their function, but it may also be that the choice of these devices by the language-learner (i.e., the choice of grammar on the basis of data) may be independent, to a significant extent, of conditions of meaning and use. If we could specify the extent precisely, the working hypothesis would become a true empirical hypothesis. Such an effort may be premature. It does, however, seem noteworthy that the extensive studies of meaning and use that have been undertaken in recent years have not — if the foregoing analysis is correct — given any serious indication that questions of meaning and use are involved in the functioning or choice of grammars in ways beyond those considered in the earliest speculations about these matters, say in Chomsky (1957).

There is, of course, no doubt that language is designed for use. The study of language form will ultimately find its place in a broader framework that will incorporate considerations of meaning and use, just as the study of grammar will ultimately find its place in a richer investigation of how knowledge of language is acquired. I believe that the work that I have been discussing here will prove to be of lasting impact and importance, whether its general hypotheses turn out to be correct or not, in that it has redirected the attention of linguists to a wide range of semantic considerations that must be integrated into the general theory of language. These questions have been disregarded for far too long, and the study of language can surely be advanced and enriched by serious concern for these topics, as is illustrated by much of the work that I have reviewed.

Very roughly, this seems to me a fair assessment of the state of the theory of transformational generative grammar — at the moment. Obviously, any such assessment must be quite tentative and imprecise at crucial points. I will be very surprised if in a similar review several years from now, or perhaps next week, I will not want to present a rather different picture — surprised, and not a little disappointed as well.

REFERENCES*

Akmajian, A.
   1968   "On the analysis of cleft sentences".
Bowers, J. S.
   1968   "Adjectives and adverbs in English".

* Published items are identified by date of publication, unpublished items by date of appearance. Therefore the dates do not always indicate order of original appearance.

200

SOME EMPIRICAL ISSUES

1969 "Surface structure interpretation in English superlatives".
1970 "A note on remind".

Bresnan, J.
1970 "On sentence stress and syntactic transformations".
Chomsky, N.
1957 Syntactic Structures (Mouton).
1964 "Current issues in Linguistic theory", H. Lunt (ed.), Proceedings of the IXth International Congress of Linguists (Mouton); revised version, J. Fodor and J. J. Katz (eds.), The Structure of Language: Readings in the Philosophy of Language (Prentice-Hall); futher revised version (Mouton), 1964.
1965 Aspects of the Theory of Syntax (M.I.T Press).
1967 "Remarks on Nominalization".
1968a Language and Mind (Harcourt-Brace).
1968b "Deep structure, surface structure, and semantic interpretation". See also this volume, p. 60-117.
1970 "Remarks on Nominalization", Readings in English Transformational Grammar, Jacobs and Rosenbaum, eds. (Ginn and Co.). See also this volume, p. 9-58.
Chomsky, N. and M. Halle
1968 The Sound Pattern of English (Harper and Row).
Culicover, P.
1970 "Syntactic and Semantic investigations"
Dougherty, R. C.
1968 "A transformational grammar of coordinate conjoined structures", M.I.T Ph.D. dissertation.
1970 "A grammar of coordinate conjoined structures", Language 46:4.
forthcoming. "Review of Bach and Harms (eds.), Universals in Linguistic Theory", Foundations of Language,
Emonds, J. E.
1969 "Root and structure-preserving transformations", Ph.D. dissertation. M.I.T.
Fillmore, C.
1968 "The case for case", Universals of Language, E. Bach and R.T. Harms (eds.) (Holt, Rinehart and Winston).
1969 "Verbs of judging: an exercise in semantic description", Papers in Linguistics, A.L. Vanek (ed.), 1:1.
Fodor, J.
1969 "Three reasons for not deriving 'kill' from 'cause to die'".
Gruber, J.
1965 "Studies in lexical relations", Ph.D. dissertation, M.I.T.
Halle, M.
1959 The Sound Pattern of Russian (Mouton).
Jackendoff, R. S.
1969 "Some rules of semantic interpretation for English", Ph.D. dissertation, M.I.T.
Katz, J. J.
1966 The Philosophy of Language (Harper and Row).

1967   "Recent issues in semantic theory", *Foundations of Language*, Vol. 3, pp. 124-194.

f.c.   "Generative semantics is interpretive semantics"

Katz, J. J. and Paul M. Postal
1964   *An Integrated Theory of Linguistic Descriptions* (M.I.T Press).

Kimball, J.
1969   "*Remind* remains".

Lakoff, G.
1968   "On instrumental adverbs and the concept of deep structure", *Foundations of Language* 4, 4-29.
1969a   "Presuppositions and relative grammaticality", *Studies in Philosophical Linguistics*, W. Todd (ed.), Series one.
1969b   "On derivational constraints", *Papers from the Fifth Regional Meeting*, Chicago Linguistic Society, R. I. Binnick *et al.* (eds.).
1969c   "On generative semantics".

Lakoff, G. and J. R. Ross
1969   "Another case of propositional negation", *Phonetics Laboratory Notes*, Vol. 4, University of Michigan.

Lees, R. B.
1960   *The Grammar of English Nomalizations* (Mouton).

Matthews, G. H.
1968   "Le cas échéant".

McCawley, J. D.
1968a   "The role of semantics in a grammar", *Universals of Language*, E. Bach and R.T. Harms (eds.) (Holt, Rinehart and Winston).
1968b   "Lexical insertion in a transformational grammar without deep structure", *Papers from the Fourth Regional Meeting*, Chicago Linguistic Society.
1969c   "Tense and time reference in English".

Morgan, J. L.
1969   "On arguing about semantics", *Papers in Linguistics*, A.L. Vanek (ed.), 1:1.

Perlmutter, D.
1968   "Deep and surface structure constraints in syntax", Ph.D. dissertation, M.I.T.

Postal, P. M.
1968   *Aspects of Phonological Theory* (Harper and Row.)
1969a   "Anaphoric islands", *Papers from the Fifth Regional Meeting*, Chicago Linguistic Society, R. I. Binnick *et al.* (eds.).
1969b   "On the surface verb *remind*".

Ross, J. R.
1967   "Constraints on variables in syntax", Ph. D. dissertation, M.I.T.
1968a   "On declarative sentences".
1969a   "Auxiliaries as main verbs", *Studies in Philosophical Linguistics*, W. Todd (ed.), Series one.
1969b   "Guess who?", *Papers from the Fifth Regional Meeting*, Chicago Linguistic Society, R.I. Binnick *et al.* (eds.).

Selkirk, L.
1970 "On the determiner systems of noun phrase and adjective phrase".
Weinreich, U.
1966 "Explorations in semantic theory", *Current Trends in Linguistics*, Vol. III, T.A. Sebeok (ed.) (Mouton).

INDEX OF NAMES

INDEX OF TERMS

acceptability, 27-29, 132
active, 34, 35, 104, 175, 180
adequacy, descriptive, 125-129, 161
adequacy, explanatory, 127, 129, 161
agent, 43, 46, 72, 74, 75, 155, 172, 175, 176
agent-postposing, 41-47
alienable, 37, 38
Aspect, 16

base, 12-16, 21, 23, 30, 34, 46, 48, 49, 52, 85, 103, 113, 138, 156, 162

causative, 24, 25, 26, 59, 72, 150, 159, 171
competence, 11, 71, 115
component, categorial, 12-14, 16, 21, 30, 34, 65, 66, 71, 81, 84, 101, 103, 114, 115, 131, 138
component, transformational, 13-15, 17, 80
constraint, derivational, 126, 133, 139-141, 181-183, 185, 194, 195, 197, 198

Deep structure,
  See : Structure, deep

entry, lexical, 12, 21, 22, 38, 39, 64, 66, 71, 72, 74, 75, 146, 154, 169, 171, 173
Evaluation measure,
  See : measure, evaluation

Evaluation procedure,
  See : Procedure, evaluation

Feature, contextual, 21, 36, 38, 39, 41, 66, 131
Feature, semantic, 19, 22, 130, 135
Feature, syntactic, 5, 17, 21, 21, 39, 48, 54, 130, 135, 142, 143, 160
Filtering function,
  See : function, filtering
Function, filtering, 65, 109, 116

generic, 157, 158, 168
grammar, 11, 12-14, 27-29, 48, 49, 52, 59, 62-66, 68, 70, 71, 73, 74, 78, 79, 85, 89, 100, 101, 103, 114, 115, 117, 120-122, 124-130, 133, 138, 150, 157, 160, 161, 170, 172, 173, 180, 182, 184, 185, 190, 192, 198, 199
grammar, case, 174, 175, 178
grammar, context-free, 12, 131, 198
grammar, transformational, 17, 49, 75, 120, 125, 133, 141
grammar, universal, 11, 13, 15, 17, 124, 161
grammaticalness, 27, 120

hypothesis, extended lexical, 150, 151
hypothesis, lexicalist, 5, 18, 22-24, 26, 27, 29, 36, 38, 39, 41-44, 52, 54, 55, 57-60, 162-165